"Bury Me Not in a Land of Slaves"

The author's great grandparents: Martha Ball Dobson and Samuel Dobson, a free black family of Charleston, South Carolina

"Bury Me Not in a Land of Slaves"

African-Americans in the Time of Reconstruction

Joyce Hansen

Franklin Watts
A Division of Grolier Publishing
New York   London   Hong Kong   Sydney
Danbury, Connecticut

Interior Design: Kathleen Santini

Visit Franklin Watts on the Internet at:
http://publishing.grolier.com

Library of Congress Cataloging-in-Publication Data

Hansen, Joyce.
   "Bury me not in a land of slaves." African-Americans in the time of Reconstruction / by Joyce Hansen.
      p. cm.
   Includes bibliographical references (p.) and index.
   Summary: An account of African-American life in the period of Reconstruction following the Civil War, based on first-person narratives, contemporary documents, and other historical sources.
   ISBN: 0-531-11539-9 (lib. bdg.)   0-531-16463-2 (pbk.)
      1. Afro-Americans—History—1863-1877—Juvenile literature. 2. Afro-Americans—Social conditions—19th century—Juvenile literature. 3. Freedom—United States—History—19th century—Juvenile literature 4. Reconstruction—Juvenile literature. 5. United States—Race relations—Juvenile literature. [1. Afro-Americans—Social conditions—19th century. 2. Race relations. 3. Reconstruction.] I. Title

E185.2.H32 2000
973'.0496073—dc21

99-030040

GROLIER
PUBLISHING

Contents

Bury Me in a Free Land

Make me a grave where'er you will,
In a lowly plain, or a lofty hill;
Make it among earth's humblest graves,
But not in a land where men are slaves.

❧ ❧ ❧

I ask no monument, proud and high,
To arrest the gaze of the passers-by;
All that my yearning spirit craves,
Is bury me not in a land of slaves.

Frances E. W. Harper

Introduction

I, young in life, by seeming cruel fate,
Was snatched from Afric's fancied happy state.
What pangs excruciating must molest,
What sorrows labor in my parent's breast!
                                                    Phillis Wheatley

In 1619, twenty African men and women, captives on a Dutch vessel "manned by pirates and thieves," arrived in Jamestown, Virginia. The pirates had attacked a Spanish ship headed for the Caribbean and stolen the Africans from the Spaniards. They traded the captives, like pieces of cargo, to the Virginia colony for food. Some historians see this incident as the place where the long, bitter history of Africans in America began—simply . . . quietly . . . accidentally—perhaps a twist of fate.[1]

The Africans remained in Jamestown, settling into the life of the British colony. We do not know much about them except that two, Antony and Isabella, married and had a boy they named William. Records also show that these first Africans in English America were defined not as slaves, but as servants.[2] A fixed system of slavery had not yet taken hold in the American economy and the American imagination.

Antony, Isabella, and the other Africans became part of the established system of indentured servitude in which poor white immigrants sold their labor for a period of years. "Under this system thousands of whites—paupers, ne'er-do-wells, religious dissenters, waifs, prisoners, and prostitutes—were shipped to the colonies and sold to the highest bidder. Some were sold, as the first black people were sold, by the captains of ships. Some were kidnapped on the streets of London and Bristol, as the first black people were kidnapped in the forests of Africa."[3]

In 1619 a Dutch ship brought a cargo of captured Africans to the American colonies, landing at Jamestown.

For the next thirty to forty years, whites and blacks in the colonies labored and lived under the same colonial laws. A few of these people of color became landowners and planters, which gave them the right to vote. And some even purchased the labor of indentured servants—both black and white.[4] How and why, then, did things change? Why were laws enacted that forced men and women of African descent either into a system of lifelong slavery, or into a form of semifreedom, in which they were denied the rights and privileges of the whites?

By the end of the 1630s in Virginia, laws establishing lifelong African slavery began to replace the system of indentured servitude.[5] Merchants and planters found that importing and enslaving Africans was more profitable and economical than buying indentured servants. The hovels of Europe could not supply the increasing number of laborers needed to work the growing farms and plantations, especially those in the southern colonies. Also, indentured servants were often troublesome and could not always be absolutely controlled. Servants had some protection under colonial laws, and could complain to a magistrate or judge about a cruel master. Indentured servants—unlike black Africans—could run away before completing their terms and blend into the free white population. And, finally, an indentured servant could become the former master's business competitor once the term of indenture was completed.

Technological advances also contributed to the fate of millions of Africans in America. England's industrial revolution in the late 1700s, coupled with the invention of the cotton gin in 1793, generated a greater demand for cotton. Planters with capital accumulated land and slaves and increased their cotton production. New England business owners outfitted ships and imported Africans from the Caribbean and Africa. The African slave trade and its ancillary businesses—manufacturing, ship building, and importing and exporting products—helped to create the wealth of a nation.

Captive Africans—enslaved for life, far from their original birthplaces, unable to run away to their homes, unable to run anywhere because they could not blend into the population (although some Africans escaped to Native American settlements), stripped of all political rights—were the perfect subjects for a cruel system that would ultimately tear apart a nation.

This advertisement for the sale of Africans was posted in Boston about 1700.

American slavery lasted for more than two hundred years, persisting long after the colonies won their independence and formed a new nation founded on the principles of freedom and democracy. Most enslaved men and women lived in the South, where they provided the labor on tobacco farms and on sugar, rice, and cotton plantations. But African slave labor was also employed in northern colonies. Slaves worked farms in Rhode Island, Connecticut, and New York. Enslaved workers were found in Boston, Charleston, New York, and other

Slaves provided the labor on sugar, rice, and cotton plantations, and on tobacco farms, as seen here in an 1750 engraving showing the processing of tobacco by slaves and workers.

colonial cities. Some were skilled craftsmen—carpenters or blacksmiths—serving their owner's business. Sometimes a skilled slave artisan was the owner's most valuable possession. In the late 1600s, Richard Elliott petitioned the New York City Council to pardon two of his slaves accused of a crime. He stated that he had many children to support and depended on the two slaves he had trained as coopers—to make and repair wooden casks and tubs.[6]

Slaves and their children were considered property and had few, if any, rights. Some slaveholders tried to keep families together; however, economic considerations took precedence over love between a mother and child or a man and a woman. Slaves were property, and if a slaveholder needed capital or had to pay a debt, their family and emotional relationships were not considered. Marriages among enslaved men and women were not legally recognized.

Enslaved children had little or no schooling. In some states it was against the law to teach a slave to read and write. Slaves could not own property, could not sue or testify in court, could not leave the plantations or farms where they worked without a pass, and could not protest inhuman punishment. The slave owners had absolute power. Yet slaves resisted. There were revolts on slave ships; there was armed rebellion, especially in the Caribbean, where blacks outnumbered whites; and everywhere, slaves ran away. (During the Revolutionary War, an estimated 100,000 slaves freed themselves by running to the British lines.)[7]

Enslaved people struggled against the chains that bound them. Those chains held fast for two hundred years, and were broken only by a catastrophic civil war that divided the nation.

1. A House Divided

I do not expect the Union to be dissolved—
I do not expect the house to fall—
but I do expect it to cease to be divided.
                                    Abraham Lincoln[1]

When the Revolutionary War ended in 1783, some northern and middle states took steps to end slavery and prohibit their citizens from participating in the slave trade. The Massachusetts courts abolished slavery, and Connecticut and Rhode Island instituted a system of gradual emancipation in 1784. New York and New Jersey also gradually freed its enslaved population, beginning in 1785 and 1786. Pennsylvania had begun to emancipate its slaves as early as 1780. The federal government prohibited slavery in the Northwest Territory (present-day Ohio, Indiana, Illinois, Michigan, and Wisconsin) in 1787.[1]

In 1787, many of the delegates attending the Constitutional Convention in Philadelphia thought that slavery would gradually die a natural death—especially if importing new slaves was outlawed. Delegate Luther Martin of Maryland declared that the "slave trade was inconsistent with the principles of the revolution, and dishonorable to the American character." Another delegate warned that God would judge the nation because of slavery.[2] Moral considerations, however, took second place to economic concerns. Charles Pinckney of South Carolina reminded the delegation that more slaves meant the country could produce more goods. Another South Carolina delegate, Edward Rutledge, said, "If the Northern States consult their interest, they will not oppose the increase of slaves, which will increase the commodities of which they will become the carriers." In other words, northern business interests also benefited from the slave trade.[3] Oliver Ellsworth, a Connecticut delegate, agreed. "What enriches a part enriches the whole," he declared.[4]

14

The peculiar "Domestic Institutions of our Southern brethren."

Selling a Mother from her Child.

Mothers with young Children at work in the field.

A Woman chained to a Girl, and a Man in irons at work in the field.

"They can't take care of themselves"; explained in an interesting article.

Hunting Slaves with dogs and guns. A Slave drowned by the laws.

Servility of the Northern States in arresting and returning fugitive Slaves.

Abolitionist societies sponsored lectures and published books and newspapers to gain support. The front page of the antislavery newspaper, Emancipator, of September 2, 1839, portrayed the evils of slavery.

Throughout the slavery debate, delegates from Georgia and South Carolina insisted that if they were not allowed to import slaves, they could not approve the Constitution. Roger Sherman of Connecticut may have spoken for many delegates when he stated that "it was better to let the Southern States import slaves than to part with those states."[5]

Thus, instead of abolishing slavery within the new republic, a compromise was reached: The importation of slaves would be allowed until 1808. The delegates then made another significant decision. As they discussed how each state's population would be represented in Congress, they devised the three-fifths compromise. Three-fifths of the slaves in the state's population would be counted, for purposes of taxation and representation. The Constitution was ratified in 1788.

As the nation expanded in the nineteenth century, the controversy over whether new territory would be slave or free grew as well, sparking regional and national disputes. The northern and free states had more industry and were less dependent on slave labor. They feared that southern states, with large numbers of slaves,would have more representation and therefore more power in Congress because of the three-fifths compromise. Animosity between slave and free states intensified each time new territory was acquired. More fuel was added to the slavery controversy by the abolitionists—members of a reform movement to abolish slavery, along with sexism and racism.

By the 1850s the controversy over slavery was reaching a crisis. In Kansas, proslavery and antislavery forces battled so violently the region was called "bleeding Kansas." The Fugitive Slave Act of 1850 allowed escaped slaves to be returned to their owners even if they had reached the free states. People caught harboring or helping slaves were fined, and U.S. marshals were used, along with slave hunters, to capture runaway slaves in free territory.[6]

In 1857 the slavery question reached the Supreme Court. Dred Scott, a Missouri slave, had lived in Illinois, a free state, and in Wisconsin, a free territory. Scott sued his owner for freedom, claiming that since he'd lived in a free territory, he should be declared free. Presiding justice Roger B. Taney ruled that because Scott was born a slave, he was not a citizen of the United States and residence in a free territory did not make him free. The majority opinion of the Supreme Court also stated that the Congress did not have the power to bar slavery from a territory.[7] This ruling incensed abolitionists and other northerners who feared the spread of slavery to the territories. It offered no hope for the slaves.

The years of dissension and crisis reached a climax when Abraham Lincoln was elected president in 1860 and South Carolina seceded from the Union at the end of the year. Ten other southern states followed. Southerners felt that because their interests and their way of life were so different from that of the north, they could no longer be part of the Union. In February 1861, southern delegates meeting in Montgomery, Alabama, formed the Confederate States of America and elected Jefferson Davis as the president.

Neither the North nor the South wanted a war, but Abraham Lincoln declared that the "Union of these states is perpetual, a marriage bond that cannot be broken." None of the states had the right to defy federal authority and leave the Union. Jefferson Davis, however, evoking the words and spirit of the Declaration of Independence, said that "governments rest on the consent of the governed."

On April 12, 1861, the Confederacy bombarded Fort Sumter in Charleston Harbor and the American Civil War began. However, President Lincoln made it clear that Federal troops were fighting southerners not to free slaves, but to save the Union. "If I could save the Union without freeing any slaves, I would do it and if I could save it by freeing *all* the slaves, I would do it; and if I could save it by freeing some and leaving others alone I would also do that. What I do about slavery, and the colored race, I do because I believe it helps to save the Union."[8]

Abraham Lincoln believed slavery was morally wrong, but he knew that most northerners would not go to war just to free enslaved blacks. The abolitionists, however, insisted that the war was about slavery. And many enslaved people thought that slavery was the cause of the conflict. As soon as the war began, large numbers of slaves who lived near a Union fort or camp began running to the Union lines.

The first of what would become a flood of fugitive slaves escaping to the Union army appeared on a May evening in 1861, just a month after the firing on Fort Sumter. Three black men, slaves working on Confederate fortifications near Norfolk, Virginia, slipped away to nearby Fortress Monroe

By 1863, large numbers of freedman had come into the Union Army lines. This scene is in North Carolina.

and asked for refuge. Army policy at that time required commanders to turn away fugitive slaves. But Benjamin Butler, the fort commander, let them stay and put them to work. Since the slaves were enemy property, they could be considered contraband of war—valuable enemy property that could be used for the benefit of the Union. More and more slaves followed. By July about nine hundred men, women, and children were living at the fort. Those who could work were employed and received small compensation.

By 1862 Abraham Lincoln and his advisers were aware that the South had a mighty force in its slave manpower. The Confederate army, with thousands of slaves at its disposal, could relieve its soldiers from grueling fatigue duty. Slave labor built fortifications, repaired roads, cleaned campsites, cared for horses, and buried the dead. The slaves also worked the fields to provide food for the army and the civilian population. An article in the Alabama *Advertiser* in 1861 outlined the military importance of slaves.

> *The total white population of the eleven states now comprising the Confederacy is 5,000,000, and therefore, to fill up the ranks of the proposed army, 600,000, about 10 percent of the entire white population, will be required. In any other country than our own such a draft could not be met, but the Southern states can furnish that number of men, and still not leave the material interest of the country in a suffering condition.*

The writer added that slavery "is really one of the most effective weapons employed against the Union by the South."[9]

A strike against slavery, Lincoln felt, would weaken the Confederacy, and so he signed the Emancipation Proclamation in 1863. It declared that slaves in the states in rebellion were freed. Because the proclamation was a military measure, however, it did not free slaves in the four border states—Kentucky, Maryland, Delaware, and Missouri. Those states were still in the Union, and the North did not want to antagonize them. Freeing their enslaved population would disrupt their economies. Lincoln feared the border states might then join the Confederacy.

An 1865 drawing shows Abraham Lincoln proclaiming Emancipation to a grateful nation.

The Emancipation Proclamation was a first step in the journey to freedom. It did not free all slaves, but it gave enslaved men and women in the Confederate states an opportunity to seize their freedom. It stated that Union military commanders could employ fugitive slaves and that black men would be accepted into the Union army. As Union troops captured Confederate territory, the numbers of black refugees swelled. About 180,000 black men fought for their freedom in the Civil War and approximately 500,000 people freed themselves by running to the Union forces.[10] They settled into camps and were employed by the military to dig trenches, bury the dead, build breastworks, and perform other fatigue duty. Black women worked as nurses and laundresses. For most of these black laborers, it was the first time that they were paid for their labor.

However, refuge with the army did not mean complete freedom. The war was not yet won, and there was still no clear policy as to how, or even if, the former slaves would become part of the nation. Abraham Lincoln explored the idea of resettling the freed men and women in Panama or on the Ile à Vache, near Haiti. The president and his advisers discussed the cost of such a massive project but abandoned the idea because of the expense and because, as one adviser reminded Lincoln, of the need for black laborers in the states.

Finally, on April 9, 1865, when Confederate general Robert E. Lee surrendered at the Appomattox Courthouse in Virginia, the war was over and four million enslaved men, women, and children were freed. How would they begin to create and build new lives?

Brief Biography
PHILLIS WHEATLEY

The drawing of Phillis Wheatley appeared opposite the title page of her book of poems published in London in 1773.

Phillis Wheatley's short, bittersweet life reflects the early colonial period when some black people were able to throw off the shackles of slavery. In 1761, a slave ship sailing from the Senegal–Gambia region of West Africa arrived in Boston, Massachusetts, and unloaded its human cargo.

The wife of a merchant-tailor, Susannah Wheatley, went to the Boston slave market looking for a young girl to be a personal servant. Mrs. Wheatley was in poor health and needed help. She saw a young girl of about six or seven, wrapped in a dirty piece of carpet. She looked frail, but there was "something so gentle and modest in the expression of her dark countenance," Mrs. Wheatley said.[1] She purchased the frightened child and took her home.

Mrs. Wheatley bathed her and gave her clothing and a new name, Phillis. She and her daughter, Mary, began teaching Phillis to speak English. They were amazed at how quickly she learned and extended their lessons to reading.

Massachusetts, unlike some other states, had no laws forbidding a slave to learn to read and write. After a year and a half, "Phillis not only learned to speak English correctly, but she was able to read fluently in any part of the Bible." The girl remembered nothing of her past. "She could not tell how long it was since the slave-traders tore her from her parents, nor where she had been since that time."[2] Phillis's only

21

memory of Africa was her mother pouring out water to the rising sun every morning.

When Mrs. Wheatley noticed that Phillis tried "to make letters with charcoal on the walls and fences," she instructed her in other subjects.[3] Phillis studied geography, history, Latin, and her favorite subject, English poetry. When she was about fourteen, she began to compose verses. At seventeen, her first poem was published: "A Poem, by Phillis, A Negro Girl, in Boston, on the Death of the Reverend George Whitefield."

When Phillis was about nineteen she traveled to London with Mrs. Wheatley's son, and became a celebrity when her book, *Poems on Various Subjects, Religious and Moral*, was published there in 1773. One of her most famous poems was "His Excellency General Washington," written in 1775. She was the second woman in colonial America and the first African-American woman to have her work published.

At some point the Wheatley family freed Phillis. When Susannah Wheatley became ill, Phillis returned to Boston to be with her. She died in 1774, and her husband died four years later, followed by the death of their daughter. In April 1778, Phillis married a free black man, John Peters. She continued to write, although her new poems were not published. This was the period of the American Revolution, and times were hard. According to some accounts, her husband had difficulty making a living. Phillis worked in a boardinghouse until her health failed. Her first two children died, and she passed away in abject poverty, along with her third child, on December 5, 1784, when she was probably about thirty-one.

Although Phillis Wheatley's life was short, her poet's voice was not silenced, and we can still hear her words. How many other poets died— their voices stilled in the holds of slave ships and muted in cotton fields?

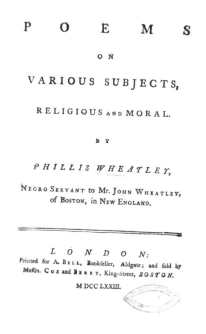

22

2. Free at Last

Everybody was proud to be free.
They shouted and sung.
                    Wylie Nealy,
                    Former slave

It was nine o'clock in the evening and a blazing bonfire lit the woods surrounding the Lester Plantation in Florida. People from the Lester place as well as from neighboring plantations were drawn to the light. They came from every direction, knowing that it signaled a meeting. A host of people crowded silently together in the shadows of the fire.

The trunk of a fallen pine tree became a stage, and hopeful eyes followed Richard Edwards as he stepped up on it. Edwards, like most of his audience, had once been enslaved. He was a gifted speaker and used his ability in those first months after the Emancipation Proclamation to help his fellow freed men and women make the transition from slavery to freedom. Now, as the torches flickered, chirping crickets and other insects created a background chorus, accompanying Edwards's strong voice.

My brothers and my sisters, the text I have ready for you is this: Glory Hallelujah! Not such a great while ago we couldn't-a had such a gathering as this. We belonged to the white man and he said when we could go and where we could go. . . . if we went out without permission, with no pass, we risk meeting up with the patter-roller [patroller, slave catcher], and if we gets caught, we gets whipped. The black man can go where he pleases now! He ain't got no master—and the white man ain't got no slave—Glory, glory hallelujah!

There's one more thing, brothers and sisters. You ain't, none of you, going to feel real free till you shake the dust of the Old Plantation off your feet and go to a new place where you can live out of sight of the great house. So long as the shadow of the great house falls across you, you ain't going to feel like no free man or woman. You must all move clear away from the old places you know. . . .Take your freedom, my brothers and sisters. You-all is just as good as anybody and you is just as free . . . stand up on your feet—lift your eyes— and shout with me Glory, Hallelujah! Amen![1]

Slave quarters on a southern plantation

With slavery officially and completely abolished, how would the freed men and women respond? No doubt many acted as Richard Edwards advised. They left the "shadow of the great house" in individual ways and at various times during 1865, the first year of freedom.

Some responded as did the former slaves of Gertrude and Jefferson Thomas of Georgia. The couple owned property in Augusta and a plantation outside of the city. When northern troops entered Augusta on May 1, 1865, Jefferson Thomas knew that the day he'd dreaded since the war began had arrived. He summoned his former house slaves, and he and his wife gazed at the familiar faces that had once been their human property—thousands of dollars of investments in slaves now lost. Their valuable property was free.

Gertrude Thomas had mentioned the slaves time and again in her diary: Daniel, the first slave Jefferson had owned, had been a wedding present from his father. She remembered the scene of her father-in-law lifting the small boy so that he could go with the newlyweds in their buggy. He had been a loved and loyal slave. Betsy, a smart girl who was learning to be an excellent servant. Aunt Sarah, who cooked the family's meals. Nancy, who did the washing and ironing. There were others too—Willy and Manly and Manly's two children, along with Patsy and another child named Frank.

Now Jefferson Thomas told the former slaves that they were free but that he would pay them for their labor if they remained. "I would as soon pay you wages, as anyone else."

No shouting or celebration followed Jefferson's announcement. The servants went back to work. Gertrude and Jefferson Thomas were puzzled, not knowing what to expect from their former slaves. However, Gertrude Thomas kept a watchful eye on them. She made an observation in her diary about the general mood of the freed men and women in the area. "Excitement rules the hour," she wrote. "No one appears to have a settled plan of action. The Negroes crowd the streets and loaf around the pumps and corners. . . ."

Gertrude Thomas took comfort in the fact that her servants had not seemed to change. Then, several days later, Daniel, their favorite and most faithful servant, was gone. He had left the night before without saying goodbye. Gertrude Thomas could not understand why Daniel left without a word. "If he returns to the yard he shall not enter it," she declared in her diary.

A nineteenth-century engraving shows blacks leaving the plantation in search of freedom.

The next day Betsy left the house to buy the paper. Gertrude Thomas thought nothing of it—Betsy picked up the paper every day. After a longer time than usual had passed, Gertrude Thomas asked another servant about Betsy. When the servant told her that Betsy had taken her clothes out of the ironing room to wash them, Gertrude Thomas knew that Betsy would never return.

The Thomases learned later that Betsy and her mother, who lived on the Thomas plantation outside of Augusta, had planned their disappearance. Betsy's mother "left the plantation, came up and took Betsy home with her," Mrs. Thomas wrote in her diary. "I felt interest in Betsy, she was a bright quick child and raised in our family would have become a good servant. As it is she will be under her mother's influence and run wild in the streets."

Sarah left a few days after Betsy. Nancy, who had been doing the washing and ironing, was told to take over Sarah's job and cook too. But Nancy left also, taking her two children with her. The Thomases' offer of clothing and a salary of twenty-five cents a week did not tempt Willy to stay, and he too departed. The following day, Manly and his two children were gone. Gertrude and Jefferson Thomas realized that a way of life had ended; yet they felt betrayed as their former slaves left, one by one. One diary entry from the end of May, 1865 reflects this feeling, as Gertrude Thomas describes Susan, a woman who had been with the family since Gertrude herself was a child:

> *I am under too many obligations to Susan to have hard feelings towards her. During six confinements [pregnancies] Susan has been with me, the best of servants, rendering the most efficient help. To Ma she has always been invaluable and in cases of sickness there was no one like Susan. Her husband Anthony was one of the first to leave the Cuming Plantation and incited others to do the same. I expect he influenced Susan. . . . I have often heard Pa say that in case of a revolt among Negroes he thought that Susan would serve as ringleader. She was the first servant to leave Ma's yard and left without one word.[2]*

Even though the Thomases had lived intimately with their house slaves and cared deeply for some, they would not or could not see them as men and women with the same needs and desires that they had. They could not understand why Betsy would prefer to be with her own mother rather than remain a servant in the Thomas household. Or why faithful and dependable people like Susan and Daniel would leave the only "home" they'd ever known without saying goodbye.

The human spirit catches onto notions like freedom and democracy. Susan, Daniel, Sarah, Willy, and Nancy lived in a democracy—though they were enslaved. They had observed what it was like to be free, for they had lived among free people. They most likely knew a lot more about the war and impending emancipation than the Thomases had thought possible. Overheard conversations, news from slaves on other plantations, secretly learning how to read, were some of the ways in which enslaved people found out about the world beyond the farm or plantation. Sarah and Susan, Nancy

"Talking About Freedom" was the title of this scene on a southern cotton plantation.

and Betsy, Daniel and Willy, had five years to prepare for freedom. When the time came, they calmly left the "shadow of the great house."

"Shaking the dust of the plantation off their feet" was a physical as well as a symbolic act. A woman who had been the cook in a South Carolina home for many years left to be a cook for a neighboring family. Her former owners offered her more money if she would stay. The woman refused, saying, "If I stay here, I'll never know I am free."[3]

Freely coming and going without a written pass or permission was a significant test of freedom. Henry Adams walked away from the plantation in Louisiana he had lived on because he wanted to "see whether I am free by going without a pass."[4] Before emancipation, black people, even those who were "free," could not go from one place to another without either written passes identifying their owners and destinations, or certificates stating that they were free. Patrollers—citizen patrols composed mainly of poor white men who owned neither land or slaves—were actually vigilantes, sometimes hired by planters to search for runaway slaves, investigate planned slave insurrections, break up secret meetings among slaves, and check passes of blacks found outside the plantation. The patrollers also dispensed punishment. These vigilantes were the among the most feared and hated symbols of slavery.

Andrew Boone, enslaved on a North Carolina plantation, recalled a time when the patrollers caught a fellow slave. "Sam Joyner, a slave, belonged to Marster. He was runnin' from de patterrollers and he fell in a ole well. De patterroller went after Marster. Marster told 'em to get ole Sam out and whip him. . . ."[5]

The simple act of strolling down a road had a profound meaning for freed men and women; however, the most compelling reason for taking to the road as soon as slavery ended was the desire to be reunited with loved ones.

Brief Biography
FREDERICK DOUGLASS

An engraved portrait of the author appeared in Narrative of the Life of Frederick Douglass, An American Slave, *published in 1845.*

Frederick Douglass was born into slavery in Talbot County, Maryland, near Chesapeake Bay, in 1818. He would become one of the most famous and effective leaders in the antislavery movement.

When Douglass was eight, he was sent to Baltimore, Maryland, to serve in the household of his master's brother, Hugh Auld. Auld's wife, Sophia, became fond of the youngster and began to teach him the alphabet until her husband stopped her. It would spoil the child Auld declared, and make him an unfit slave; but the seed had been sown. Frederick was determined to learn to read and write fluently. "The first step had been taken," he said. "Mistress, in teaching me the alphabet, had given me the *inch*, and no precaution could prevent me from taking the *ell* [a measure of length]." [1]

Frederick secretly taught himself to read and write. In 1838, at twenty, he fled to the North. Anna Murray, a free black woman who would become his wife, and a number of abolitionists—some black, some white—in New York City and Massachusetts helped him escape. He settled in New Bedford, Massachusetts, and began his life's work as an abolitionist, orator, journalist, and writer.

The abolitionists often used the first-hand testimony of escaped slaves to expose the horrors of slavery. Douglass was an ideal spokesperson for the abolitionist cause. He was impressive, with a thick head of hair, tall and handsome. His eloquent speeches held his audiences spellbound. On August 16, 1841, in Nantucket, Massachusetts, Douglass spoke publicly for the first time. After Douglass's speech recounting his experiences as a slave, the abolitionist leader and publisher William Lloyd Garrison rose and shouted from the audience, "Shall such a man be held a slave in a Christian land?"[2]

Douglass became an agent of the Massachusetts antislavery society that same year. In 1845, he wrote his powerful autobiography, *Narrative of the Life of Frederick Douglass, an American Slave, Written by Himself.* More than 30,000 copies of the book were sold in its first five years.[3] After its publication, abolitionist leaders arranged for Douglass to tour and lecture in England, delivering antislavery speeches.

Although Douglass was gaining fame on both sides of the Atlantic, he was still a fugitive and in danger. Because of the fugitive slave laws, he could be captured and sent back to his owner, Thomas Auld, if he returned to America. Friends in Britain raised money so that Douglass could purchase his freedom. Auld received $1,250.00, and Douglass returned to America in 1847 as a free man. He then began a career in journalism.

The first issue of his antislavery newspaper, *The North Star,* was published on December 3, 1847 in Rochester, New York. The paper became an important publication in the abolitionist cause; however Douglass was not concerned only with slaves in the South, but also with the conditions for blacks in the North and other regions. Free blacks often faced racism and prejudice. In Philadelphia between 1832 and 1849, there were riots in which whites killed black people and destroyed their churches and homes.[4] During the Civil War, white draft protestors took part in antiblack riots in New York City. The Colored Orphan Asylum was burned to the ground during three days of rioting. Slave catchers were another threat for men and women of color in northern cities. Douglass was warned when he reached New York to be wary of kidnappers.

Free blacks had few political and civil rights. Before the Civil War, they could vote only in Massachusetts, Maine, Vermont, New Hampshire, and Rhode Island. New territories admitted into the Union did not give black people the franchise. Massachusetts was the only state to allow blacks to sit on a jury.[5] Blacks also had few economic opportunities. When the government offered land grants to settlers in the New Mexico and Oregon territories, they were for whites only.[6] And in many cases black children attended separate schools. For example, the African Free School had been established for black youngsters in New York City in 1786.

Douglass believed that prejudice would end when slavery was finally abolished. He met with other black men at conventions to discuss the problems of northern blacks. Although these black conventions had no legal force, the individuals who attended began to think and speak about important national issues that affected black people. They were training grounds, too, for black leadership. In 1853, concern over the fugitive slave act and other problems brought 140 delegates from nine states to Rochester, New York, where Frederick Douglass led the meeting. The participants discussed establishing a "manual labor college" for black youngsters.[7]

Douglass continued his autobiographical writing with *My Bondage, My Freedom*, published in 1855. During the Civil War, Douglass's was one of the insistent voices declaring that the war was about slavery. He recruited blacks for the Union army. Douglass also provided leadership during the difficult Reconstruction era.

In 1881, he wrote *The Life and Times of Frederick Douglass*. In his later years he became president of the Freedmen's Bank, received political appointments, and remained a loyal Republican. He was appointed marshal, 1877-81; recorder of deeds for the District of Columbia, 1881-86; and Minister to Haiti, 1889-91. He died at his home, Cedar Hill, in Anacostia, near Washington, D.C., in 1895. He was one of the most venerated black leaders of the nineteenth century.

NARRATIVE

OF THE

LIFE

OF

FREDERICK DOUGLASS,

AN

AMERICAN SLAVE.

WRITTEN BY HIMSELF.

BOSTON:
PUBLISHED AT THE ANTI-SLAVERY OFFICE.
No. 25 CORNHILL
1845.

3. Ties that Bind

One day one of my uncles named Wash Sheppard
come and tried to get me to go live with him. He say
he wanted to get the family all together again.
                    Morris Sheppard,
                    Voices From Slavery

Mary, a black woman about seventeen years old, stared sadly at the white couple standing before her. Olivia and William Adams had been her master and mistress. She had cared for the couple's babies and spun clothing for the family since she was ten years old.

Olivia Adams, crying and wiping her tears, handed the girl a basket packed with food. She warned Mary to be careful because it was rough in Texas, where Mary was headed. She gave Mary a second basket, this one filled with clothing. William Adams put one arm around his sobbing wife and handed Mary manumission papers containing a formal release from slavery, with the gold seal of the state of Missouri. The Emancipation Proclamation did not apply to slaves in Missouri, for the state belonged to the Union. Adams, however, may have felt that slavery's days were numbered—that once the war was ended, all slaves would be freed. He freed his five hundred slaves, including Mary, in 1863. But he advised Mary to keep her papers with her at all times because they were her only proof that she was free.

Mary boarded a steamboat to go down the Mississippi River to New Orleans—the first leg of her long journey to Texas. She regretted leaving, but she was eager to find her mother who had belonged to Olivia Adams's parents and had been taken along when they moved to Texas in 1856.

After New Orleans, Mary boarded two more steamers—first one to Galveston, Texas, and then another to Houston. From Houston, she traveled

Setting out for a new life after the war—a drawing from the Reconstruction period

by stagecoach for two days to Austin. It was there that her troubles really began.

She had no idea where to find her mother. As she walked the dusty streets, looking into the face of every black woman she saw, a white man approached her.

"Where're you going?" he asked

"I'm looking for my mother."

"Come on with me," the man ordered.

Mary followed, thinking that he would help her; however, he took her to a slave auction, put her on the auction block, and asked for bids. Mary remembered what Will Adams had told her. She stood calmly as people bid,

This "freedom paper" issued by a justice of the peace stated that the bearer, Reverend John F. Cook of Washington, D.C., and his two children were free. The tin container was used to protect the document.

and after she was sold to the highest bidder, Mary pulled out her papers and held them up for everyone to see.

Charley Crosby, the purchaser, said, "Let me see them."

"You just look at it up here," Mary snapped, backing away.

"This gal is free," the man said, squinting closely at Mary's papers. By this time she had no money left and had not found her mother. She went home with Crosby and lived in the quarter with his slaves and was paid a small amount of money for working for him. When the war ended in 1865, Mary resumed her search.

Mary's story ended happily. She found her mother in Wharton County, Texas.

"Talk about crying and singing and crying some more, we sure done it. I stays with Mama till I gets married in 1871 to John Armstrong."[1]

To many white observers, people like Mary Armstrong looked like idle vagrants. "The [N]egroes are rambling about the country," wrote a South Carolina planter in 1865. "The colored population is so nomadic, it is almost impossible to report them accurately,"[2] said the rector of a South Carolina church.

The sight of black men and women whose lives they could no longer control was unsettling to many planters and their families. What may have unnerved them the most was the evidence that their former property had minds, wills, and hearts. Former slaveholders often watched in bewilderment, as a flood of black humanity clogged the dusty southern roads searching for lost loved ones.

Some people found family members quickly and easily because a relative lived on a neighboring plantation. Or various members of a slaveholding family held slaves who were related, as in the case of Mary Armstrong. Therefore, siblings and parents, while not living in the same household, at least knew where their loved ones were.

Freed people traveled many miles and through a number of states to locate family. A northern journalist in North Carolina reported meeting a freedman who had walked almost 600 miles searching for the wife and children that he'd lost when he was sold away from them. Another couple, Ben and Betty Dodson, begged their owner to sell them together, but he refused. They met twenty years later in a refugee camp after the war. "This is my Betty sure," Ben said. "I found you at last. I hunted and hunted till I track you up here. "[3]

Most freed slaves, however, were not as fortunate. Black newspapers founded in the South after the war were filled with requests for information about missing persons.[4] The *South Carolina Leader* began its "Information" column with the following: "Persons wishing information of their relatives can have them advertised one month for two dollars and a half." These notices appeared in a variety of newspapers:

Information Wanted of Moses Watkins, who was sold from W. Rob't Watkins. When last heard of he belonged to Mr. Robert McWhorter,

*5 miles from Woodville on the Athens Branch Railroad. If he is
living, he is about 20 years of age and of dark complexion. Also,
Abraham Watkins, of the same family. Last heard of he was in Maryland,
Dist, City of Memphis, Tenn., aged about 18 years, dark complexion.
Any information regarding either will be thankfully received at the office
of this paper.*

Fanny Watkins

*Information wanted of my children, Daniel, Susan, and Mary Tate. When
last heard from, they were with Mr. John Luke, of Clarke County, Va.
Any information addressed to me at No. 243 Currant Alley, Philadelphia,
will be thankfully received.*

Daniel Tate

*$200 Reward. During the year 1849, Thomas Sample carried away from
this city as his slaves our daughter, Polly and son, George Washington, to the
State of Mississippi and subsequently, to Texas, and when was last heard from
they were in Lagrange, Texas. We will give $200.00 each for them, to any
person who will assist them, or either of them, to get to Nashville, or get word
to us of their whereabouts, if they are alive. Any information concerning them
left in this city, at our place, so that we can get it, will be liberally rewarded.*

*Ben East
Flora East*

Poignant pleas for information about loved ones appeared in black newspapers as late as the 1880s. It was difficult for parents to find children who had been taken away from them. Often the search was long, painful, and unsuccessful, especially if the youngster had been removed to another state.

A child who was taken away when very young might not remember a parent or a previous home. Often the parent could not recognize an older child last seen years earlier. If the child's name was changed, as new owners often did, then it was almost impossible for a parent to find the young son or daughter who had vanished in the changes of time. Frankie Goole had always lived with her white mistress, even sleeping in her room. The mistress was the only "mother" Frankie had known, as her birth mother had been sold away

On some plantations a slave child might grow up alongside the owner's children, as portrayed in an 1860s drawing of "Domestic Life in South Carolina."

when she was a baby. When the war ended, Frankie's mother came to find her child who was now twelve. She went before a judge to gain custody but when the judge asked Frankie whether the woman was her mother, Frankie said, "I don't know, she says she is."[5]

Often on large plantations, some slave children were taken to be raised in the master's house. Sarah Debro, who lived on a plantation in North Carolina, was taken from her mother and raised by her mistress and trained to be a maid. Sarah's mother cried when Sarah was taken away. She knew her child would never be allowed to live with her in their cabin again.

Sarah became accustomed to life at the Big House. "My dresses an' aprons was starched stiff. I had a clean apron every day. We had white sheets on the beds and we . . . had plenty to eat too, even ham. When Mis' Polly went to ride she took me in the carriage with her. . . . I loved Mis' Polly." When Sarah's mother came to get her after the war, the girl clung to her former mistress. Polly begged the mother to let her keep Sarah. Sarah's mother refused and took her distraught daughter with her.[6]

In some cases a former slaveholder tried to keep a child away from a parent. Their old master tried to hide Millie Randall and her brother Benny from their mother, who had to go to court get them back.[7]

After emancipation in 1865, some former slaveholders took advantage of apprenticeship laws that allowed children between ten and fourteen to be "bound" to an adult. The bound youngster was fed, housed, and taught a craft or skill. In a system similar to indentured servitude, the child remained with the craftsworker or in the family, working until he or she was twenty-one years of age. A strong, healthy boy or girl could provide years of labor as an apprentice. In many cases, these children were not taught a skill, but were used as laborers.

Silas Dothrum was ten when freedom came to Arkansas. Silas had never known his parents, who were deceased or had been sold away. Emancipation did not change the boy's life. "They kept me in bondage, and a girl that used to be with them," he recalled. "We were bound to them [so we had] to stay with them. They kept me just the same as under bondage. I wasn't allowed no kind of say-so."[8]

Finding loved ones, however, was only the beginning in the efforts to build a new life out of the ashes of slavery and the chaos of war.

4. The Coming Day

One ever feels his twoness—an American, a Negro,
two souls, two thoughts, two unreconciled strivings,
two warring ideals in one dark body, whose dogged strength alone
keeps it from being torn asunder

W. E. B. Du Bois

Enslaved men and women tried to maintain family ties, but marriage between slaves was not granted the legal standing that it had among free Americans. "What God has joined together, let no man tear asunder" did not apply to slave unions. When slavery ended, legalizing "slave marriages" was an important step toward building a family

Slaves in the All Saints Parish of the low country of South Carolina had been allowed to be married by clergy. The slave owners in this rice-growing region, where the plantations were large and slaves outnumbered whites, tried to keep slave families intact. They believed this was the most efficient way to keep control. Historian Charles W. Joyner wrote: "In promoting for each slave a stake in the social order through marriage, they discouraged runaways far more effectively than the threat—and example—of dire punishment could."[1]

However, these marriages were not recognized by the state of South Carolina or any other state. A slave could not enter into a legal contract, and marriage is a contract. If a slave owner fell on hard times and wanted to separate a couple to sell them for more money, the slave marriage meant nothing.

Many enslaved couples remained faithful, even when separated for years. A number of men and women who were together when they were emancipated went to a magistrate or justice of the peace to legalize their unions under state laws.

Elizabeth Hyde Botume, a teacher in a freedmen's school in South Carolina, described the legalization of slave marriages.

In the days of slavery the marriage relation amongst the [N]egroes was rarely held too sacred to be broken by the wishes of the masters or mistresses.... All the people in our district had lived together according to the old slave code, as husbands and wives.

Amongst the first persons who came forward to be married were Smart and Mary Washington who had lived together over forty years. . . . Others came forward to have the ceremony performed, and get the certificate, for which they had profound respect. . . . One evening four couples came to the schoolhouse to meet "the parson" who was to perform the marriage ceremony for them. They came straight from the field, in their working-clothes. . . . [2]

The solemnization of a marriage, the search for family, for work, and a home, were all part of the search for a new self in a changed world. Another significant representation of self is a name. One of the first things that the enslaved Africans had lost on farms and plantations were their ancestral names based on ethnic and cultural ties.

Among some West African people, names are given according to when the child is born. Among others, the name might include the family's traditional village or region, or a child might be named according to birth order. An eldest daughter's name could indicate that she was the firstborn. Once enslaved, the descendants were called simply John or Mary, and their connection was not to an ancestral home or region, but to their owner's plantation.

Parents usually named their own children, but some plantation masters or mistresses insisted on naming a slave child. The youngster then would have two first names: one used by the master and the other used by the child's family and friends. Sabe Rutledge, a slave on a South Carolina rice plantation, was called Newman by his master, but Sabe, an African name, by his friends and family. [3]

After the war, the federal government told the freed people, many of whom had just one name, that they had to have surnames. A good number took the name of the owner of the plantation where they lived at the time of emancipation. Some who had been sold and resold many times chose the name of the owner of the plantation where they had been born. Others chose the family name from a plantation where they'd lived with other kin, hoping that it would help missing relatives locate them. Some freed men and women refused to take the names of former masters and mistresses, instead choosing a name to represent their new freedom.

In his *Narrative*, Frederick Douglass described how he chose a name after he escaped from Maryland.

> *We now began to feel a degree of safety, and to prepare ourselves for the duties and responsibilities of a life of freedom. On the morning after our arrival at New Bedford . . . the question arose as to what name I should be called by. . . . I gave Mr. Johnson the privilege of choosing me a name, but told him he must not take from me the name of "Frederick." I must hold on to that, to preserve a sense of my identity.*[4]

Although many of the men and women held in slavery made swift and drastic changes, just as many did not immediately leave their houses of bondage. The very old and the very young were the weakest of the freed population. If the young had no birth parents or other family to take them away, they remained where they had been. The elderly who had no children to care for them and carry them away also remained. A number of older people who stayed celebrated freedom for their children and grandchildren; for themselves, freedom had come too late. Their strength gone, their labor used to enrich someone else's vineyard, they remained where they were, especially if their former owners were humane and allowed them to stay. "Old Amelia and her two grandchildren . . . I must support them as long as I have anything to give," the South Carolina planter Henry W. Ravenel wrote in his diary in 1865.

There were instances, too, of the reverse situation. A former slave would find the same humane spirit in his or her soul and remain to take care of a sick and elderly master or mistress. Elisha Doc Garey said that his widowed former mistress begged him and his fellow slaves to stay, for she could not run the plantation without them. They remained, out of sympathy for her.

A number of people remained on the plantations and farms because they had no place to go, or they wanted to see what was happening amid all the confusion and changes. Also, many people stayed on plantations after the war if the planter had not lost his land and needed laborers. The freed people and the planters realized that a crew of experienced field hands could mean the difference between survival and financial ruin for a planter. These men and women performed all the labor—from building homes, caring for animals, to raising crops—and could bargain and make demands of their onetime masters and mistresses.

Some demanded and received plots of land. Others demanded that their employer build a plantation school. Sometimes, instead of a monthly salary, the laborer worked as a sharecropper, receiving a share of the crop.

Thousands of others, however, did not leave immediately because no one told them that slavery had ended. Isolated on plantations in interior regions of Georgia, South Carolina, and especially Texas, their lives went on. They were kept away from outside influences and were at the mercy of patrollers if they tried to run. A freedman from Chester County, South Carolina, said that the only news they had received from their master was purposely misleading, and he and other enslaved men and women didn't learn they were free for two years after the war.[5]

A sharecropper's cottage near Richmond, Virginia, about 1870

When New Orleans fell to the Union troops in 1862, planters in Mississippi and Louisiana moved more than 125,000 slaves to Texas, away from the war and away from the opportunity to escape to Union lines.[6] Since no major battles were fought in Texas, planters there managed to isolate their people, keeping away all news of emancipation. Susan Merritt was a girl in Texas when she and the other slaves found out that they were free. "I hears about freedom in September [1865] . . . a white man rides up to Massa's house on a big, white hoss . . . a government man. He have the big book and a bunch [of] papers."[7]

The "government man," probably a military officer, wanted to know why the people had not been told they were free. The planter replied that he was trying to get his crop out. The government official told the men and women on the plantation that they were no longer enslaved. The planter promised them twenty acres and a mule if they stayed and worked. They stayed, but received neither mules nor land.[8]

Most black residents of Texas didn't learn about their emancipation until June 19, 1865. The freedmen and freed women then had their own emancipation celebration known as "Juneteenth." The day is still celebrated in various African-American communities around the country.

The reactions to freedom were as varied as the freed people themselves. The road they traveled on their journey to freedom depended upon the experiences they'd had during slavery, their physical and emotional state, and their natural abilities and talents. Finding their children and kin, choosing names, solidifying relationships through marriage, and deciding for the first time where they would live and work were important steps. But as the freed people began to carve out places for themselves, they discovered that difficult times lay ahead. They learned, as Frederick Douglass had cautioned, that "the work does not end with the abolition of slavery, but only begins."

W. E. B. Du Bois

W. E. B. Du Bois was born in 1868 in Great Barrington, Massachusetts, when the Civil War was still a raw memory for many Americans, and Reconstruction of the South was in its earliest stages.

Du Bois grew up in the tightly knit community of Great Barrington, along with a few other black families who had settled in the region after the American Revolution. One of his earliest known ancestors was a man named Tom, born about 1730 in West Africa, who was kidnapped and enslaved as a child. He served the Burghardt family, living with them in Berkshire County, Massachusetts. Tom joined the Berkshire County Regiment during the Revolutionary War. He received his freedom and a land grant when the war ended and began to raise his own family, which prospered well into the nineteenth century.

Du Bois's upbringing was secure and nourishing in a close family with a strong emphasis on education. His intellectual skills were evident at an early age. The youngest student and the only African-American in his senior class, he graduated with honors at Great Barrington High School in 1884. Du Bois said that though he was the only black student, he did not feel any differences between himself and the white students until he reached his teen years and "there the differences were comparatively small."[1]

However, when Du Bois entered Fisk University in 1885 at the age of seventeen, he stepped into a different world. Fisk, in Nashville, Tennessee, was established in 1866 to educate African-American students. Du Bois studied and socialized with fellow students, but was appalled by the total racial segregation outside of the college walls. "No one but a Negro going into the South without previous experience of color caste can have any conception of its barbarism."[2]

Experiencing a world that was still deeply steeped in the racism and violence of slavery, war, and Reconstruction, Du Bois found the work that would consume him spiritually and intellectually for the rest of his long and productive life. This respected historian, educator, writer, editor, scholar, sociologist, and political activist has been called "the father of serious black thought."[3]

Du Bois's landmark studies and books were a foundation for future historians and scholars of African and African-American life and culture. He was one of the first scholars to seriously study people of African descent in America. He did advanced academic work at Harvard University, where he earned a doctorate in history, and at the University of Berlin in Germany, where he continued his studies in history and sociology. In

1896 his doctoral thesis, *The Suppression of the African Slave Trade to the United States 1638-1870*, was published as the first volume of the series called the Harvard Historical Studies. In it, Du Bois traced the unsuccessful efforts of the United States to end the slave trade.

His scientific approach is apparent in his highly praised study *The*

*In November 1910, Du Bois launched a national monthly magazine—*The Crisis*— to focus on international relations. It was published by the newly formed National Association for the Advancement of Colored People.*

46

Philadelphia Negro, published in 1899, which analyzed the problems of Philadelphia's black community. He studied the community while teaching at the University of Pennsylvania. In 1903, Du Bois moved away from objective, scientific work to write *The Souls of Black Folk*, a series of essays exploring the complexity of African-American life. The book is still in print and is a source of inspiration to contemporary writers, artists, and intellectuals.

His study, *Black Reconstruction in America*, was at first dismissed by critics. In this 1935 work, Du Bois rejected white historians' earlier studies claiming that Reconstruction was one of the most corrupt periods in American history. Reconstruction had been depicted as an era when unscrupulous northern capitalists manipulated ignorant ex-slaves and inflicted untold suffering on the conquered white people of the South. Du Bois's interpretation of Reconstruction places black people at the center of the effort to rebuild the South and overcome the legacy of slavery. Modern historians have since reassessed this era, and Du Bois's seminal study has influenced their reinterpretations. Along with scholarly research, Du Bois wrote poetry, novels, and numerous articles and essays.

After a lifetime of struggle to end racism, battling both white racists and other black intellectuals and leaders who thought he was too radical, Du Bois became a citizen of Ghana, in West Africa, in 1959. After receiving his Ghanaian naturalization papers Du Bois wrote:

> *My great-grandfather was carried away in chains from the Gulf of Guinea. I have returned that my dust shall mingle with the dust of my forefathers. There is not much time left for me. But now, my life will flow on in the vigorous young stream of Ghanaian life which lifts the African Personality to its proper place among men. And I shall not have lived and worked in vain.*[4]

William Edward Burghardt Du Bois died in Accra, Ghana, in 1963 at the age of ninety-five. His living was not in vain.

5. The Freedmen's Bureau

The Freedmen's Bureau was the most
extraordinary and far reaching institution
of social uplift that America has ever attempted.
W. E. B. Du Bois

Before Congress adjourned in March 1865, it passed a bill creating the Bureau of Refugees, Freedmen, and Abandoned Lands, commonly known as the Freedmen's Bureau. Congress also chartered the Freedmen's Savings Bank, to encourage the former slaves to save part of their earnings.[1]

Because the Freedmen's Bureau was organized by the War Department, its commissioner and other personnel were drawn from the army. Abraham Lincoln chose General Oliver Otis Howard as its head. Howard was appointed commissioner of the Freedmen's Bureau by President Andrew Johnson on May 12, 1865, a month after Lincoln's assassination.

The young general from Maine was liked by people working to help the freedmen after the war. He was called a "Christian soldier" and a "pious gentleman." Du Bois wrote in *Black Reconstruction*, "The most fortunate thing that Lincoln gave the Bureau was its head, Oliver Howard. Howard was neither a great administrator nor a great man, but he was a good man. He was sympathetic and humane, and tried with endless application and desperate sacrifice to do a hard, thankless duty."[2] The work of the bureau was hard duty indeed. Du Bois pointed out that "nothing is more convenient than to heap on the Freedmen's Bureau all the evils of that evil day, and damn it utterly for every mistake and blunder that was made."[3]

Bureau headquarters were established in a home in Washington, D.C., that had belonged to a senator who had defected to the Confederacy. Commissioner Howard organized the bureau into four divisions: l) abandoned lands under

In a drawing of a scene in North Carolina, a Union General from the Freedmen's Bureau tells the former slaves of their rights voted by Congress.

government control; 2) records, which included labor, schools, food rations, and "commissary supplies"; 3) financial; and 4) medical.[4] Assistant commissioners who were responsible for specific regions of the South and local agents who supervised districts within the regions were chosen to begin the daily operations. In some regions, the bureau inherited tasks that the army had been performing: settling people in refugee camps and making certain that the freedmen were paid for their labor.

More than any other organization or government agency, the Freedmen's Bureau was responsible for supervising the transition from a system of slave labor to one of free labor. Bureau agents negotiated labor contracts between former slaves and former masters, making certain that the freedmen received fair wages, and settled disputes between planters and laborers. When necessary, the bureau interceded in civil court cases to ensure that blacks received equal justice. The bureau resettled people on farms and plantations where laborers were needed and placed people temporarily on abandoned land.

A bureau agent's life was often as dangerous as it was difficult. For many southerners, the Freedmen's Bureau symbolized northern oppression. In a report to Commissioner Howard on conditions in North Carolina an inspector wrote: "I had an interview with Governor Worth and other prominent citizens. They all expressed a desire that the Bureau be withdrawn. . . . they desire to conduct their own affairs in their own way. They expressed the belief that the Negroes would be well treated by the people of the State." Knowing that fair treatment of blacks was unlikely, the inspector advised that, "until perfect equality under the laws is established, and provisions made for the support of the destitute, this opinion is not well grounded."[5]

An 1880 lithograph offers an optimistic view of the changes in the South. The scene on the left, of slavery before the war, shows an overseer with a bloodhound giving orders to a work gang. On the right, free blacks relax from their labors.

Besides protecting blacks, the agents had to appease the white community. Former slave owners and planters, having lost control over the laborers, felt demeaned. The former slaves had rights and a government agency to assist them.[6] Some agents were able to work with the white population, while protecting the freed people from abuse and exploitation.

Not all bureau agents, however, were committed to the bureau's mission. Some were cynical and war-weary ex-soldiers. Some held nineteenth-century stereotypical views about the inferiority of Africans and people of African descent. They worked with planters, local white leaders, and civil authorities to get black laborers to sign work contracts, even if the terms were unfair. They enforced vagrancy laws, arresting freed people who could not prove they were employed and had a place to live. These laws criminalized people who were going from town to town searching for relatives.

Whether a local bureau agent was successful often depended on the region. In some areas, the best that agents could hope for was that they and the freedmen would not be killed. A bureau inspector reported on attacks against a Virginia district agent: "Violently assaulted on the streets of Lexington in one or two instances, annoyed and insulted on many occasions by gangs of rowdies gathering about his office after nightfall, and daring him to come out . . . the position of this officer, alone and unaided, has been anything but . . . agreeable."

The inspector also noted that "in the more distant counties . . . there are but few freed people, and these mostly employed, but not always at sufficient wages or under fair contracts. Many of them . . . hardly know that they are free. . . ." He added that they were abused and exploited by "their former masters, and forced to eke out a scanty subsistence as best they may."[7]

Texas was particularly difficult to manage because of its size and the determination of some residents that slavery would die a hard death. Approximately 38,000 returning Confederate soldiers had to be reabsorbed and reports indicated that they were looting warehouses, plundering the state treasury, and attacking freedmen.[8]

Because federal soldiers had to establish order before the bureau could begin operation, Commissioner Howard could not assign assistant commissioners for Texas until September 1865. And even then many Texas counties remained hard to control, as shown by the events in Millican, in east-central Texas.

Millican was a shipping center, and the bureau agent could detain loads of cotton if he learned that the workers had not been fairly paid. There were constant disputes between the freedmen and the planters over fair crop division. In August 1866, Samuel G. Sloan began his duties as the bureau agent in Millican. Sloan had served in the Union army. He was assigned to Millican after the army commander in the region contacted the Texas Bureau: "Please send an agent here. It is insufferable."[9] Sloan was soon discouraged by conditions in the town. Blacks could not lodge complaints against whites, even for serious criminal offenses. Nor could they appeal to a local civil authority if they were cheated by employers or subjected to unfair labor practices. In some regions of the former Confederacy, judges, sheriffs, and other local officials had held their offices since before the war. If freedmen went before a local magistrate, their complaints were thrown out of court, or they might be threatened by physical violence. Sloan observed that "white Texans would not accept the fact that blacks had to be paid for their labor and had rights under the law. They would always be treated unjustly."[10]

Blacks were kept from sitting on juries, and all-white juries would not convict whites for crimes against blacks. Yet if a black person was accused and convicted of a crime, punishment was swift and certain. At times, punishment came before a trial. Soon after Sloan arrived in Millican, a lynch mob hanged a black man accused of rape, although there was no evidence of his guilt. With no army troops nearby to protect the freedmen, Sloan could do nothing, except direct the freedmen's complaints to the local sheriff and other civil authorities. Not long after the lynching, another bureau official traveling through the county reported that "civil law is so much of a farce in Texas. . . . "[11]

Sloan was described as a competent agent who insisted that black laborers be paid fairly. When he left his post after seven months, Agent Edward Miller replaced him. Miller, too, reported that the sheriff and his deputies were unwilling to arrest whites; however Miller seemed to care little for the concerns of the freed people and appeared to be in league with their employers. As a Union soldier, Miller had been injured and lost an arm.[12] Perhaps this history contributed to his attitude. Perhaps it was easier to cooperate with the people who controlled the county.

Workers in a cotton field

Miller reported that whites and blacks in Millican got along well. He was concerned, however, about reprisals from the angry white citizens of Millican when he requested troops to protect blacks and Unionist whites (southern whites who had remained loyal to the Union during the war) after he removed an alcoholic justice of the peace and a corrupt deputy sheriff. He also requested that a sheriff be removed when the sheriff released the alleged killer of a black man. When Millican's blacks rose up and protested, they were arrested for rioting. This incident was the only time that Miller indicated to his superior officers that there were problems between whites and blacks in his district. When Miller left his post in 1867, he requested the removal of the four soldiers assigned to him. He said that because relations between blacks and whites were good, the soldiers were not necessary. A year later, six black men were killed when the Millican blacks tried to defend the black section of the town.

Incompetence and insensitivity were not the only problems among bureau agents. Some used their positions to buy plantations and farms or to go into business with carpetbaggers—Northerners who moved south after the Civil War. Southerners derided them, saying that they were so poor they carried all their belongings in carpetbags (travel bags made of carpet material) and moved south to plunder and steal.

Many Americans, in the North as well as in the South, felt no threat from the emancipated population in their midst as long as they remained agricultural laborers, performing the same work as when enslaved. Bureau reports focused on the employment of the freed people:

"On the 27th, in company with General Whittlesey, I went to Rock Mount. . . .the Freedmen were very industriously at work, and their employers expressed great satisfaction at the manner in which they observed their contracts."[13]

"The able-bodied freedmen are generally employed at fair contracts, averaging twelve dollars per month for farm hands, and labor is offered on railroads at good wages to all who desire it. . . ."[14]

"The condition of the freedmen in the sixth district is, so far as I had opportunity of judging, most satisfactory. Nearly all able-bodied Negroes are employed at good wages, generally by contracts which give them a fair proportion of the coming crops."[15]

No doubt the sight of black laborers working cotton filled many northern and southern hearts with pleasure. Cotton still brought profits in 1865 and 1866, and experienced labor was needed. Also, this sight was reminiscent of the past—before the war and the meddling Yankees. If blacks were kept at their old work, they wouldn't compete with free white labor. What more could they want? They were no longer enslaved, and they were being paid. And as one bureau report stated, "all the freedmen could be regularly and permanently employed at fair wages did all desire it."[16]

But for many of the freed people, the ultimate goal was to acquire land. Some laborers refused to sign contracts, preferring to work by the day because they believed that the government was going to give them land grants—as reparation for decades of labor without pay. Land was the symbol

Black farm workers collect pay tickets after a strawberry harvest.

of freedom; land on which to raise a family, to build a home, and to be independent and free of white domination. "All I want is to own four or five acres of land, that I can build me a little house on and call my home," a Mississippi freedman declared. "Give us our own land and we take care of ourselves; but without land, the old masters can hire us to starve us, as they please."[17]

Thousands of freedmen shared these sentiments. In the coastal areas of South Carolina and Georgia people had already settled on land that they thought belonged to them, following General William T. Sherman's Special Field Order Number 15, which set aside abandoned coastal lands between Jacksonville, Florida, and Charleston, South Carolina, for the freedmen.

Back in January 1865, as General Sherman's troops marched through Georgia and into South Carolina, thousands of slaves left their plantations, farms, and houses of bondage to follow the army and to free themselves. These children, women, and men quickly became a burden. Sherman and the War Department had to find a practical way to help the throngs of destitute freedmen following the army.

On January 12, 1865, in Savannah, Georgia, Sherman and Secretary of War Edwin Stanton met with twenty black ministers and church leaders to discuss what could be done. One member of the group stated, "We want to be placed on land until we are able to buy it, and make it our own." A few days later Sherman issued the field order, which gave each family forty acres of land. The army would also lend out mules, in those days a necessary farm animal.[18]

When Congress gave the Freedmen's Bureau supervision of the abandoned lands, it appeared that land grants would be given to the people who settled there under Sherman's Field Order. Then, on October 19, 1865, Commissioner Howard faced a crowd of almost 2,000 freed people jammed inside a church on Edisto Island, South Carolina, and must have felt overwhelmed by guilt. He was popular among the freedmen, who called him the "Christian general," understanding that he was committed to making the Freedmen's Bureau responsive to their needs. However, President Johnson had ordered Howard to be the bearer of bad news. He had the assignment: "to tell them that the owners of the land, their old masters, had been pardoned, and their plantations were to be given back. . . ." The planters wanted to grow cotton again and would hire the freedmen as laborers.

One black man shouted from the church balcony: "Why General Howard, why do you take away our lands? You take them from us who are true, always true to the government! You give them to our all-time enemies. This is not right."[19]

People were angry, as word spread by the "great black telegraph" from island to island and to the mainland. Some freedmen resisted. They pulled up the bridges leading to the islands and erected barricades along the docks. Men patrolled the shoreline so that no former masters could return to claim their land. On another island, armed black men refused to allow the white man who had owned the island to return.[20] Eventually, the freed men and women were evicted by the army. Many of them had no choice then but to sign labor contracts.

Despite its weaknesses and problems, the Freedmen's Bureau was the only safety net to keep the emancipated people from falling back into new forms of slavery. It also helped impoverished whites survive this time of upheaval and change. The Freedmen's Bureau dispensed 21 million rations of food, clothing, medicine, and fuel to destitute Southerners, both black and white. The bureau ran hospitals and treated more than 450,000 patients. By 1870, with the aid of missionary and other benevolent societies, the Freedmen's Bureau had helped to establish and maintain more than 4,300 schools with 247,333 students.[21]

But while the bureau tried to bring order out of confusion and chaos in those first months after the Civil War, Andrew Johnson carried out his own Reconstruction plans, which practically hurled the freed men and women back into conditions as difficult as slavery.

Brief Biography
MARTIN R. DELANEY

Martin R. Delaney was the first black to receive a commission in the U.S. Army.

Martin R. Delany was born on May 6, 1812, in what is now West Virginia. In 1868 his biographer wrote, "His pride of birth is traceable to his maternal as well as to his paternal grandfathers, native Africans." Delany claimed his paternal grandfather was a chieftain, captured in a war and sold into slavery in America; and that his maternal grandfather was an African prince from the Niger Valley region of Central Africa.[1]

Delany was a proud man who refused to compromise with racism and prejudice. Delany's father was enslaved, and his mother was free. In 1822 Delany's mother left Virginia, taking Martin and her other children, and moved to Chambersburg, Pennsylvania. Delany's father managed to purchase his freedom and joined his wife and children the following year. The family then moved to Pittsburgh, Pennsylvania. Martin Delany attended a school for black youngsters and after graduation was apprenticed to a doctor.[2]

By the 1830s the abolitionist movement captured Martin's interest. Searching to get away from the pervasive racial prejudice, Delany joined a group that supported the emigration of blacks from the United States. In these days, newspapers were an important vehicle for spreading information to large numbers of people. Therefore Delaney, eager to reach the black population, began publishing *The Mystery*, the only black newspaper published in the United States until Frederick Douglass established the *North Star*.[3] For more than a year,

Delany helped Douglass edit and sell the *North Star*, until he returned to the study of medicine.

Martin Delany and two other black men were accepted by Harvard Medical School in 1850, but they were denied admittance when white students protested. This incident and others, and the fugitive slave law that offered escaped slaves no safe haven anywhere in the nation, may have inspired Delany to write and publish in 1852 *The Condition, Elevation, Emigration, and Destiny of the Colored People of the United States*, in which he stated that blacks would have to leave America in order to live as free people. It is thought to be the first book published in the United States on black nationalism—the philosophy that blacks form a separate nation within the American nation. Delany later explained his philosophy in a letter to the abolitionist reformer William Lloyd Garrison.

Philadelphia, May 14, 1852
My Dear Sir: I thank you, most kindly, for the very favorable and generous notice you have taken of my hastily written book. . . . I am not in favor of . . . a separation of the brotherhood of mankind, and would as willingly live among white men as black, if I had an equal possession and enjoyment of privileges; but shall never be reconciled to live among them, subservient to their will. . . . Heathenism and Liberty, before Christianity and Slavery.[4]

These were bold words and thoughts in the nineteenth century—especially for a black man. Delany, practicing what he preached, moved to Chatham, Kent County, Canada, in 1856, where he practiced medicine. Many of his patients were fugitive American slaves.

Hoping to find a place for black Americans to live, Delany led an expedition to the Niger Valley in Africa, in 1859. His only novel, *Blake*, was published at this time, as weekly installments in a black magazine.

During the Civil War, Delany returned to America and recruited black soldiers for the Union army. He became a major in 1865—the first black officer in the Union army — and was among the first blacks to be Freedmen's Bureau agents. He worked for the bureau from 1865 to 1868 in Charleston and Hilton Head Island, South Carolina. He arranged work contracts and acted as arbitrator when the freedmen and the planters clashed over working conditions and contracts.

After finishing his work with the bureau, Delany lost a bid for lieutenant governor of South Carolina in 1874, and became disillusioned with Reconstruction politics. He distrusted white Northerners, claiming they took all the important positions in the reconstructed South, leaving out educated and talented blacks.

Delany left South Carolina in 1879, with his wife and six children, and returned to the North. By this time, Reconstruction was essentially over. Delany continued to write, publish, and lecture. He died in 1885 in Xenia, Ohio. Called the father of black nationalism, Martin Delany was, in many ways, a man ahead of his time.

6. The South Rises

*"Damn the Negroes.
I am fighting those traitorous
aristocrats, their masters."
Andrew Johnson, 1863*

Abraham Lincoln was not a vindictive man, and he wanted to heal the wounds of war as quickly and as painlessly as possible. There would be no hangings nor death by firing squads for the political and military leaders of the defeated Confederacy. Jefferson Davis, the Confederate president, was never tried for treason, but spent two years in federal prison and died of natural causes in 1889, at the age of eighty-one.

"The Union of these states is perpetual. . . ." Lincoln had said. As far as he was concerned, the states had never separated, even during the terrible war. He believed, as Du Bois later phrased it, "that the rebellion was a combination of disloyal persons in the states."[1]

It is not surprising, then, that Lincoln's Reconstruction plan was designed to allow the seceded states to easily rejoin the Union. On December 8, 1863, Lincoln issued his Proclamation of Amnesty and Reconstruction, granting the restoration of all rights as citizens to Southerners who took an oath of allegiance to the United States and accepted the abolition of slavery. Only high-ranking military and Confederate government officials would not be allowed to take the oath. Once 10 percent of the people in a state who had been eligible to vote in the presidential election of 1860 swore their loyalty to the United States, the voters could then elect delegates to a state convention. However, Confederate leaders and people owning property valued over $20,000 were not permitted to take the oath and had to obtain a special presidential pardon. The delegates in each state would have the task of writing a

An 1863 drawing shows blacks leaving their farm work after the Emancipation Proclamation

new state constitution—which had to abolish slavery—and organizing a new state government. Once the state rejoined the Union, it could send representatives to Congress. However, Congress would review the qualifications of the representatives before they took their seats.[2]

Abolitionists and Radical Republicans criticized the plan. It did not mention black voting rights or equal treatment under the law for the freedmen. The abolitionist Wendell Phillips said that it "frees the slave and ignores the negro."[3] Other Republicans complained that it would be too easy for former Confederates to regain power. Some members of Congress claimed that the president had taken over responsibilities that belonged to Congress. A struggle between the executive and the legislative branches of the government seemed likely as President Lincoln and the Congress attempted to reunite the nation.

In July 1864, both houses of Congress passed a bill that went further than the president's plan. The South would be occupied by troops and placed under military rule. Only when a majority (as opposed to Lincoln's 10 percent) of the white male citizens eligible to vote in a state had sworn allegiance to the United States could delegates be elected to a state convention. Before a Southerner was qualified to vote or become a convention delegate, he had to take a second loyalty oath, the "iron clad" oath, swearing that he had never supported the Confederacy.

As expected, Lincoln vetoed the Wade-Davis Bill. Sadly, the Great Emancipator was assassinated before the real battle with Congress over the difficult task of healing the nation's wounds and reconstructing the South could begin. It was, therefore, left to another man to take on the role of "emancipator." Andrew Johnson, Lincoln's vice president, became the great

Republican hope. Radical Republicans and others who thought Lincoln was too soft on the former rebels were certain that Johnson would be harsher. Everyone knew "Andy" hated the wealthy aristocracy and slaveholders; they knew that he'd been a fighter throughout his political career for the rights of the yeoman farmers, small merchants, and poor laborers of his own class.

Johnson had grown up poor in North Carolina. With his mother, brother, and stepfather (his father had died), he lived a rough life, and while in his teens, he was apprenticed to a tailor. Although young and

President Andrew Johnson

illiterate, he was determined to rise above his hardscrabble existence. He taught himself how to read while he was learning the tailoring trade. About 1826, he took his mother and ne'er-do-well stepfather with him to the mountains of Tennessee and opened a tailor shop. Here he learned the power of political activism. He and other small-time merchants broke the stranglehold that a few wealthy families had on the town of Greeneville. In 1829 Johnson ran for and won election to the town council.

Johnson knew at firsthand the unrelenting poverty poor whites— "mudsills"—suffered in the backwoods of North Carolina and Tennessee, and became their champion. From town council he rose to mayor of Greeneville, and then went on to serve in the Tennessee legislature. In 1843, Johnson was sent to Washington as a Congressional representative. He served in Congress until 1853, when he was elected governor of Tennessee and served two terms.

In 1857, at the age of forty-nine, Johnson returned to Washington as a United States senator and served until 1862. When the war erupted, Johnson stood firmly against secession, even though he was a southerner and a Democrat. When Johnson finally had to decide whether to side with the South and vote for secession from the Union (Tennessee was a slave state), or be a "traitor" to the South and reject secession, he said "Senators, I love my country; I love the Constitution . . . my blood, my existence, I would give to save this Union!"[4]

Many men in Johnson's east Tennessee region rebelled against the Confederacy and resented being drafted into the Confederate army. They saw the rebellion as a "rich man's war and a poor man's fight." Johnson was a conflicted man. He was not antislavery, and he owned slaves, yet he knew slavery kept landless, poor whites in a permanent underclass. Wages could be kept low because employers used slaves for everything from agricultural labor to skilled craftwork.[5]

Johnson said, "I am for emancipation for two reasons: first, because it is right in itself; and second, because in the emancipation of the slaves, we break down an odious and dangerous aristocracy; I think that we are freeing more whites than blacks in Tennessee."[6]

To assist poor whites, Johnson supported antislavery legislation. His Homestead Bill, passed in 1862, favored giving western land to nonslave-holding farmers. Du Bois claimed in *Black Reconstruction* that Johnson "championed free Western lands for white labor, and favored the annexation of Cuba for black slave labor."[7]

In 1864, Johnson ran with Abraham Lincoln on the National Union (Republican) ticket. Johnson served under Lincoln for only a month—March 4 to April 15, 1865—before he was catapulted into the presidency by Lincoln's assassination.

Du Bois eloquently described the "weird magic of history" that placed Andrew Johnson in the center of a crucial era in American history. He wrote that Johnson was:

> *born at the bottom of society . . . a radical defender of the poor, the landless, and the exploited. . . . Suddenly, by the weird magic of history, he becomes military dictator of a nation. He becomes the man by whom the greatest moral and economic revolution that ever took place in the United States, and perhaps in modern times, was to be put into effect. He becomes the real emancipator of four millions of black slaves, who have suffered more than anything he had experienced in his earlier days. They not only have no lands; they have not owned even their bodies, nor their clothes, nor their tools. . . .What more splendid opportunity could the champion of labor and the exploited have had to start a nation towards freedom?*[8]

Would President Johnson be the champion of labor and the exploited? Would the former tailor's apprentice who understood how it felt to be landless, poor and illiterate be able to lead a nation toward freedom for all of its people?

Since the Thirty-ninth Congress was in recess at the time of Lincoln's assassination, President Johnson had free reign for eight months. At first, he followed Lincoln's plan. It seemed, however, to his fellow Republicans that his peace would not be as soft as Lincoln's, and many of them were pleased.

Thirteenth Amendment (adopted 1865)

Section 1.
Neither slavery nor involuntary servitude, except as a punishment for crime whereof the party shall have been duly convicted, shall exist within the United States, or any place subject to their jurisdiction.

Section 2.
Congress shall have power to enforce this article by appropriate legislation.

On May 29, 1865, Johnson signed a Proclamation of Amnesty and then appointed governors for North Carolina, South Carolina, Alabama, Georgia, Mississippi, and Florida. Arkansas, Virginia, Tennessee, and Louisiana had already been accepted back into the Union under Lincoln's plan.[9]

The established order had toppled. Under the amnesty program, the once wealthy aristocrats—the people who had looked down upon the likes of Andrew Johnson—had to come to him for pardons. "Southern leaders descended upon the president; not simply the former slave barons but new representatives of the poor whites. Nine months after the Proclamation of Amnesty, 14,000 persons are said to have received pardons from the President."[10]

In the last months of 1865, Johnson pardoned so many former Confederates that extra staff had to be hired at the pardon office. Vanity may have clouded Johnson's judgment as the members of the southern aristocracy

"Southern leaders descended upon the president" —*seeking pardons.*

that he both hated and admired flocked around him, begging forgiveness and telling him that the way to restore order in the South was to form state governments as soon as possible. Some cabinet members offered the same advice. Also, Johnson's leniency toward former Confederate leaders and supporters may have been a maneuver to strengthen his political base. Once these people had their pardons and their property rights restored, they would be expected to support the president and his administration.[11]

At some point in the planning of reconstruction, Johnson missed the opportunity to be an emancipator for both the poor white and the freed black. In 1863 he had declared to a group of black Tennesseans, "I will indeed be your Moses and lead you through the Red Sea of war and bondage to a fairer future of liberty and peace." His actions in 1865 contradicted his words, as Johnson returned confiscated land to former slaveholders.

Du Bois wrote that "Johnson was transformed. From the champion of peasant labor, he saw himself as the restorer of national unity, and the benefactor and almsgiver to those very elements in the South which had formerly despised him. Of his real role as emancipator, and the one who was to give effective freedom to Negroes, he still had not the slightest idea. He could not conceive of Negroes as men."[12]

As Johnson's Reconstruction plan went into effect, the provisional state governors called for constitutional conventions. At the conventions, the delegates, many of them pardoned former Confederates, drafted state constitutions that abolished slavery. However, they replaced old slave laws with "Black Codes" that were nearly as effective in restricting the freed people. Once the delegates ratified the constitutions, then new state governments would be formed with elected representatives who could serve in Congress.

As the new congressmen from the "reconstructed" South headed to Washington for the reconvening of Congress in December 1865, it became apparent that the old southern leaders were back. Johnson's Reconstruction policies had opened the door for these resilient sons of the South to return. It must have seemed to some members of Congress—especially those who were abolitionists—that a long and bitter war had not achieved anything. And the freed men and women must have felt as if nothing had changed, as if the hope and the promise of freedom had been eroded.

7. One More River to Cross

There appears to be another popular notion in the South.... It is that the Negro exists for the special object of raising cotton, rice, and sugar for the whites.

Carl Schurz
Antislavery lecturer

The southern states reentered the Union, and southern leaders reentered public life. Because of the new Black Codes, many of the freed people feared they were reentering slavery as 1865 drew to a close.

The purpose of the Black Codes was to control the freed population and the labor they provided. Economic recovery for the South depended on the former slaves performing agricultural work, and the Codes prevented blacks from doing anything else. One South Carolina law stated that a freed man or woman had to be licensed for any occupation other than farmer or servant. Licenses were granted by a local judge and could be revoked if there was a complaint. This new law hurt the few blacks in Charleston who had always been free. Many were artisans—carpenters, dressmakers, tailors, boot makers. Now they needed licenses to pursue their trades. Another South Carolina law forbade freedmen from selling farm products without written permission from their employer. Sometimes the freed people cultivated small plots and sold the crops to supplement their small incomes.[1]

The language as well as the spirit of the South Carolina laws were reminiscent of slavery. Du Bois described some of these laws in *Black Reconstruction in America*:

> *Elaborate provision was made for contracting colored "servants" to white "masters." Their masters were given the right to whip "moderately" servants under eighteen. Others were to be whipped on authority of judicial officers. These officers were given authority to return runaway servants to their masters.[2]*

An 1868 lithograph shows Emanicpation had not succeeded in changing attitudes.

In Mississippi the Code required freed people to have a written statement each year assuring that they were gainfully employed and had a place to live. Without proof of employment and a legal address, they could be arrested for vagrancy. If they left their employment before the time stated in the work contract (usually one year), they would lose any wages they had earned.[3]

Other states followed the example of South Carolina and Mississippi. In Opelousas, Louisiana, the codes were as confining as iron shackles. Blacks could enter the town only if they were employed there. They had to have a pass from their employer stating why they were in Opelousas and how long they would stay. Opelousas also had a black curfew. If caught on the streets of Opelousas after 10 P.M. without a pass, a black would be arrested and fined five dollars, or forced to work for the town for five days. And black people could not buy or rent homes in Opelousas and could live within the town limits only if they were servants in white households.[4]

Labor contracts had been introduced by the army as they captured southern territory and were then employed by the Freedmen's Bureau. The contracts specified the term of employment—usually a year, from planting to harvest. Rates of payment were specified. Some laborers received wages, others received a share of the crop. The former slave owners used these contracts to keep control, especially if there was no Freedmen's Bureau agent to make sure the contract terms were fair. Some contracts covered the whole family, including children. Leaving an employer meant breaking a contract, and this could lead to arrest. Other contracts written by planters were, like the Black Codes, reminders of slavery. A contract might state that field hands needed an employer's permission to leave the plantation and that the laborers had to

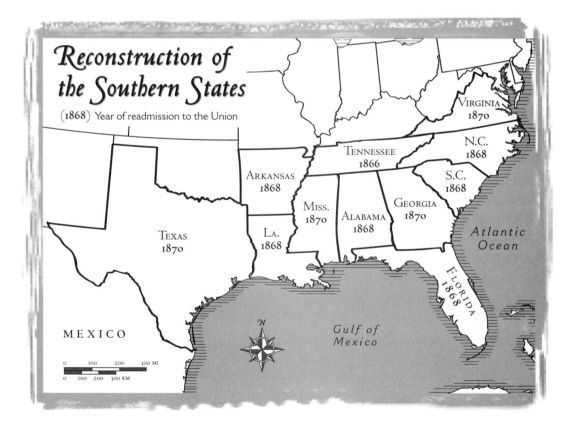

Reconstruction of the Southern States

(1868) Year of readmission to the Union

VIRGINIA 1870

N.C. 1868

TENNESSEE 1866

S.C. 1868

ARKANSAS 1868

MISS. 1870

ALABAMA 1868

GEORGIA 1870

Atlantic Ocean

TEXAS 1870

LA. 1868

FLORIDA 1868

MEXICO

Gulf of Mexico

N

0   100   200   300 MI
0   100   200   300 KM

be obedient. Most contracts required laborers to work six days a week, from ten to twelve hours a day. Contracts were in writing and were usually verified by white witnesses and approved by a judge.[5]

In some states, a white person who tried to hire away a laborer under contract to someone else was subject to a fine and imprisonment. This prevented people from leaving farms in search of more money and better working conditions. In some regions, the landowners joined together and set wages, keeping them low. When they could, the bureau agents tried to stop this wage-fixing, but it was impossible for them to cover every corner of every state.

Virginia had a strict vagrancy law. Besides the usual definition of vagrancy—an unemployed person with no known address—Virginia used another definition: a person who refused to work for the wage normally paid for the particular kind of work. Such a person could be brought before a justice of the peace and forced to work, without pay, for the county. A person who ran away from an employer could be arrested and forced to work as a prisoner, with an iron ball and chain wrapped around the ankle to restrict movement.[6]

Wages varied by state, according to how much land was still in the hands of owners and how much labor was available. Wages could be as low as twenty-five to forty cents a day. In some cases, experienced field hands were paid from five to ten dollars a month.

Even though the law in South Carolina stated that laborers could break a contract if an employer was harsh and unfair, a worker was unlikely to get a fair hearing. Although the Codes in South Carolina and some other states also said that black people could acquire property, marry, make contracts, sue or be sued, and testify in court cases involving other black people, they actually had few rights and little hope of economic or social progress.

When the Black Codes were not enough, violence was used to subjugate the freedmen. A Union general who served in Mississippi reported that an average of one black man was murdered every day, and when he traveled through his district he found seven blacks who had been "wantonly butchered."[7]

Freedmen's attempts at independence often sparked violence. When black laborers learned that slaves in nearby Harrison County had been freed, they decided to leave their plantations in Rusk County and escape to Harrison. The Rusk County planters sent slave catchers after them and the escapees were shot as they swam across the Sabine River. One witness reported that many hung from trees in the "Sabine bottom right after freedom."[8]

The future looked bleak for the emancipated men and women caught between violence and the Black Codes. Even the hope of owning land was dying. As the former Confederate states rejoined the union, their black, freed population seemed relegated to plantations and farms. One freedman bitterly described the only change on the Texas plantation where he remained after freedom, working for forty cents a day: "De same houses and some got whipped but nobody got nailed to a tree by de ears, like dey used to."[9]

When Congress reconvened in December 1865, they faced the deterioration of the peace. They realized that the South was recalcitrant, the old leaders were back in power, and the freedmen were practically back in slavery. A Mississippi planter wrote, "I will say there is not one man or woman in all the South who believes they are free, but we consider them as stolen property—stolen by the bayonets of the damnable United States government."[10]

The journey to freedom would be no easy walk.

8. New Battles

A bitter war was in progress between Congress and President Andrew Johnson over the question of the reconstruction of the states....

Congressman John R. Lynch

A strange thing happened on December 18, 1865, when the Thirty-ninth Congress convened—its first meeting since the end of the war in April. As Edward McPherson, clerk of the House, began the roll call of the representatives, he omitted the names of the newly elected congressmen from the reorganized southern states. These congressmen were, for the most part, the same men who had held power before the war.

Du Bois wrote that, "there appeared from the South, demanding seats at the opening of Congress, the Vice-President of the Confederacy, four Confederate generals, five Confederate colonels, six Confederate cabinet officers, and fifty-eight Confederate Congressmen." Thaddeus Stevens, representative from Pennsylvania, commented before the House that the South's new governments were "aggregations of white-washed rebels."[1]

Under the Constitution, the Senate and the House of Representatives have the right to review the credentials of entering congressmen. The Republicans exercised that right, refusing to seat the Southerners or to pay their living expenses while they were in the capital. One congressman said they would either "go home or starve."[2]

While Congress had been in recess, members had been observing the progress of Reconstruction. Representative Thaddeus Stevens wrote in the summer of 1865, "Is there no way to arrest the insane course of the president in reorganization? If something is not done, the president will be crowned king before Congress meets."[3]

Congress's refusal to seat the southern representatives was the first move in what would become a battle between the lawmakers and President Johnson for control of Reconstruction. Some northern leaders and politicians believed the South was not being adequately punished for its disloyalty to the Union, and should not be let back in so easily. Stories of abuses and violence against the freedmen and against Northerners who lived in the South also disturbed many people. Unionists were threatened with violence, especially if they appeared to be aiding the freedmen.

Some Republicans pointed out that President Johnson's Reconstruction policy had not dealt with the war debt, nor with the issue of representation in Congress of the reentering southern states. The number of representatives that a state sends to Congress is based on its population. How would freedmen be counted? Would each black man be counted as three-fifths of a white man, as under slavery? Or would a black man be counted as one whole person? And would black men be allowed to vote? Johnson, in a presidential paper, said that as far as he was concerned, the states were reconstructed, and issues of suffrage, or voting rights, for blacks could be left to the individual states.[4]

Most members of Congress believed that Reconstruction was their responsibility. Republicans created the Joint Committee of Fifteen—six senators and nine representatives—to review the president's policies. Twelve committee members were Republicans, and three were Democrats.[5] Both houses of Congress agreed to exclude the southern representatives until this committee investigated conditions in the states. The members were concerned about the rapid return to power of former Confederates, the reorganization of the states, and the ratification of the Thirteenth Amendment outlawing slavery, reports of violence against the freed people, and the enactment of the Black Codes.

The Congressional committee "called 144 witnesses, including 77 Northerners living in the South, 8 blacks, and 57 white Southerners. Many of the Northerners were army officers and Freedmen's Bureau officials."[6] The witnesses testified to physical violence against the freed population—a freedman shot on a plantation in South Carolina, blacks tortured for "unsatisfactory" work—pointing to the need to keep the military and the Freedmen's Bureau in the South, and the need for Congress to oversee Reconstruction.[7] When the Committee's 700-page report was completed, some people charged that it concentrated on outrages to prove its point—that presidential Reconstruction was a failure.

Added to the evidence in the report were appeals from both northern and southern black populations for full citizenship, including the right to vote. A movement to hold conventions among the free black northern populations was revived, and for the first time, black Southerners also held conventions. Blacks in the South who had always been free joined with those who were newly emancipated and organized conventions in several southern states during the turbulent first year of freedom.

On August 7, 1865, ninety-five delegates met in Nashville, Tennessee, in St. John's Chapel, African Methodist Episcopal (A.M.E.) Church. One speaker was a sergeant who had served in a black regiment in the war:

> *We shall be heard before Congress and before the legislature. . . .We want the rights guaranteed by the Infinite Architect [God]. For these rights we labor; for them we will die. We have gained one—the uniform is its badge. We want two more boxes beside the cartridge box [the right to bear arms]—the ballot box and the jury box. We shall gain them.*[8]

On September 29, the State Convention of the Colored People of North Carolina was held in Raleigh at the Loyal A.M.E. Church, with about 150 delegates. The convention's leader outlined four essential rights due black citizens: "First the right to testify in courts of justice. Second, to be received into the jury box. . . . Third, the right of colored men to act as counsel in the courts for the black man. Fourth, to carry the ballot. These are the rights we will contend for, these the rights we will have, God being our helper."[9]

On November 24, delegates meeting at Zion Presbyterian Church in Charleston, South Carolina, concluded their convention with a long written message "To The Legislature of The State of South Carolina." It began:

> *Gentlemen:—We, the colored people of the State of South Carolina, do hereby appeal to you for justice. The last four years of war have made great changes in our condition and relation to each other, as well as in the laws and institutions of our State. We were previously either slaves, or, if free, still under the pressure of laws made in the interest and for the protection of slavery.*

Among the concerns the delegates discussed in this message were the Black Codes. "We ask that those laws that have been enacted, that apply to us on account of our color, be repealed." They also sent a message to Congress requesting the right to vote, to bear arms, to sit on juries, to be judged by other black men, to acquire land, and to "protest against any code of black laws the Legislature of this state [South Carolina] may enact. . . ."[10]

Black conventions were also held in Louisiana, Virginia, and Arkansas, and in four northern states: Connecticut, Pennsylvania, Indiana, and Massachusetts.

The year 1866 brought a flurry of legislation. The Joint Committee of Fifteen submitted bills to develop rules governing the reentry of the Confederate states and to protect the fragile freedom of the emancipated population. Yet as the Republicans tried to cooperate, their ideologies and beliefs clashed. The Republican Party was divided into two major factions—radicals and moderates.

The moderates endorsed unrestricted black labor and the rights of black men and women to equal protection under the law. They welcomed the end of slavery, but did not propose black participation in government. They wanted the Republican Party to grow and become strong in the South, but they did not think that giving black men the vote could solve the party's problems. Moderate Republicans felt that fighting with the president—the head of their party—and forcing sudden and profound changes on Southerners would increase their hostility. They were willing to go along with President Johnson's policies, believing that the Republican Party could build a political base in the South by cooperating with reasonable southern leaders.

The ideas of the radical Republicans were revolutionary by nineteenth-century American standards. Many had been abolitionists and their philosophy grew from the abolitionist movement. Two of their most effective leaders were Senator Charles Sumner of Massachusetts and Representative Thaddeus Stevens of Pennsylvania. Both men, along with fellow radicals, believed that Reconstruction was the opportunity to fulfill the promise of the American Revolution—that all men are created equal and are endowed with certain rights. They believed that black men should be allowed to vote, and advocated a strong central government that could secure civil and political rights for everyone.[11]

Representative Thaddeus Stevens (left) of Pennsylvania and Senator Charles Sumner (right) of Massachusetts were leaders of the radical Republicans and attempted to shape Reconstruction policy so that the Democratic ideals on which the country was founded would become a reality for all races and all classes of Americans.

Stevens was a master politician with a sharp tongue and quick wit and never wavered from his quest to eradicate slavery. He worked to get allotments of 40 acres for each former slave and was bitterly disappointed when his plan failed.

Sumner used his intellect and his gift of oratory to secure equal pay for black soldiers who served in the Civil War and to get legislation passed to end discriminatory practices in federal courts.

In January 1866, the committee submitted its first piece of Reconstruction legislation to Congress—a bill to continue the work of the Freedmen's Bureau. President Johnson vetoed it, saying it was too expensive, used military courts in peacetime, and was not needed. One congressman noted that it was unusual for the president to veto such an important bill. "It came as a shock to Congress and the country. Excitement reigned supreme," he said.[12]

Excitement reigned supreme for a long time as Congress and the president battled. On February 5, 1866, Sumner, especially disliked by the president, stood up in the Senate to make one of his moving and scholarly speeches. The hall was packed. The galleries were filled with black visitors, including many in Washington to attend the Colored National Convention organized by Frederick Douglass and other black leaders. Douglass was in the audience, along with Henry Highland Garnet, a black minister active in the antislavery struggle. The black audience was eager to hear one of the few powerful white voices speaking for the rights of people of color.

Sumner was fifty-five years old and described as "handsome, but heavy of carriage, a scholar and gentleman. . . ." The huge hall was silent as he spoke.[13]

> *I begin by expressing a heartfelt aspiration that the day may soon come when the states lately in rebellion may be received again into the copartnership of political power and the full fellowship of the Union. But I see too well that it is vain to expect this day, which is so much longed for, until we have obtained that security for the future, which is found only in the Equal Rights of All, whether in the courtroom or at the ballot box. This is the Great Guarantee without which all other guarantees will fail. This is the sole solution of our present troubles and anxieties. This is the only sufficient assurance of peace and reconciliation. . . .[14]*

Some fellow senators called Sumner arrogant and stubborn, but he was a hero to the freed people.[15] Several days later, a delegation attending the Colored National Convention met with the president to urge him to consider black suffrage. Frederick Douglass and his son Lewis, Henry Highland Garnet, and several other black men informed the president that they represented "the colored people of the States of Illinois, Wisconsin, Alabama, Mississippi, Florida, South Carolina, North Carolina, Virginia, Maryland,

Pennsylvania, New York, New England States, and District of Columbia." Frederick Douglass addressed the President:

> *Your noble and humane predecessor placed in our hands the sword to assist in saving the nation, and we do hope that you, his able successor, will favorably regard the placing in our hands the ballot with which to save ourselves. . . . The fact that we are the subjects of Government, and subject to taxation, subject to volunteer in the service of the country, subject to being drafted, subject to bear the burdens of the State, makes it not improper that we should ask to share in the privileges of this condition.[16]*

The president gave his usual response: "It is the people of the States that must for themselves determine this thing. I do not want to be engaged in a work that will commence a war of races."[17]

Douglass attempted to convince the president that one way to avoid a race war was to give blacks the vote. Johnson suggested that black leaders should convince the "colored people" that they would be better off if they lived "elsewhere than crowded right down there in the South. . . ."

Douglass reminded the president that blacks could not move freely because of the Black Codes: "There are six days in the year that the Negro is free in the South now, and his master [employer] then decides for him where he shall go, where he shall work, how much he shall work—in fact, he is divested of all political power. He is absolutely in the hands of those men."

The president: "If the master now controls him or his action, would he not control him in his vote?"

Douglass: "Let the Negro once understand that he has an organic right to vote, and he will raise up a party in the Southern States among the poor, who will rally with him. There is this conflict that you speak of between the wealthy slaveholder and the poor man."

The president: "there is this conflict, and hence I suggest emigration. If he cannot get employment in the South, he has it in his power to go where he can get it."[18]

The meeting ended with the president's suggestion that blacks leave the country. Most blacks did not wish to emigrate. They were born in the United States and had played a major role in building the nation. Black leaders would continue to press for equal rights and the franchise.

9. Congress Acts

The whole fabric of Southern society must be changed, and it can never be done if this opportunity is lost.
Congressman Thaddeus Stevens

The Joint Committee of Fifteen resubmitted the bill to extend the life of the Freedmen's Bureau, hoping to override the president's veto. The bill passed in the House, but not the Senate; however the radicals were as determined as the president. They continued to create legislation to give blacks civil and political rights, including the right to vote. Congress wrote the Civil Rights Act, granting citizenship to all persons born in the United States regardless of race or color. It also provided for the punishment of anyone who deprived a citizen of civil rights, including the right to make contracts; to sue; to give evidence; to inherit, buy, sell, own, or transfer property; and to be subject to the same laws and punishments as white citizens.[1]

Johnson vetoed the bill on March 27, 1866. He claimed it would allow Chinese, Native Americans, and Gypsies to become citizens along with blacks. Referring to the freedmen he said, "Four million of them have just emerged from slavery into freedom. Can it be reasonably supposed that they possess the

Civil Rights Act – 1866

Blacks *"shall have the same right in every State and Territory in the United States to make and enforce contracts; to sue, be parties and give evidence; to inherit, purchase, lease, sell, hold, and convey real and personal property; and to full and equal benefit of all laws and proceedings for the security of person and property as is enjoyed by the white citizens, and shall be subject to like punishment, pains and penalties, and to none other, any law, statute, ordinance, regulation, or custom, to the contrary notwithstanding."*
From: Black Reconstruction in America, 1860-1880,
W. E. B. Du Bois

80

An engraving from Harper's Weekly *showed crowds celebrating outside the galleries of the House of Representatives after the Civil Rights Act of 1866 was passed.*

requisite qualifications to entitle them to all the privileges and equalities of citizens of the United States?"[2]

Two weeks later, both houses of Congress passed the Civil Rights Act over the president's veto—Congress was beginning to weaken the president's authority. Concerned that the act could be repealed or recalled, some congressmen proposed a set of resolutions that eventually became the Fourteenth Amendment to the Constitution. The amendment defined citizenship and prevented states from denying basic civil rights—the right to life, liberty, property, and equality under the law. It also prohibited from holding office anyone who had taken an oath to serve the country—government officials—and then joined the Confederacy. The resolution also denied claims for compensation for loss of property (slaves) because of emancipation. Confederate states had to ratify the Fourteenth Amendment before they could rejoin the Union.[3]

While Congress and the president battled, with Congress passing bills and the president vetoing them, two race riots shocked the nation. The first occurred in Memphis, Tennessee, on April 30, 1866. The city had been on edge since the war ended and destitute black refugees poured into Memphis. The city enforced vagrancy laws. At times police arrested blacks who were innocent of any crime.

Fighting broke out between black soldiers recently mustered out of the army and local police after soldiers stopped the police from arresting a black man. A three-day riot resulted. Whites burned homes, churches, and schools in the black section of the city. More than forty blacks and two whites were killed. Over eighty people were wounded.

When the local Freedmen's Bureau agent asked the army commander stationed nearby to intervene, he refused, saying that "he had a large amount of public property to guard." He also said that he couldn't trust his troops to defend the freedmen because they "hated Negroes too."[4]

On July 30, another riot broke out in New Orleans, Louisiana. Even during slavery, New Orleans had a large, and politically active, free black population. A constitutional convention had been convened to work out political issues. Blacks attended the convention as observers only. A group of

Newspapers published this drawing showing the burning of a freedmen's school in Memphis during the riot in 1866.

black laborers paraded in front of the convention hall demanding the right to vote. When angry whites attacked them, the two groups fought in the streets. People inside the convention hall were attacked when they tried to leave. Forty-eight people died, and 166 were wounded. A congressional inquiry called the incident a "massacre."[5] Perhaps as a result of the unrest after these tragic events, Congress was able to override the president's veto of the Freedmen's Bill, and it was passed in July, extending the life of the bureau until "abolished by law."[6]

But President Andrew Johnson was a determined man. Later, a congressman recalled his impressions of Johnson:

> *There were two striking points in Johnson's character, and I knew him well: first, his loyalty to the Union, and second, his utter fearlessness of character. He could not be cowed, old Ben Wade, Sumner, Stevens, all the great leaders of that day could not, through fear, influence him one particle. . . . He sought rather than avoided a fight. Headstrong, domineering, having fought his way . . . from the class of so-called "low whites" to the highest position in the United States, he did not readily yield to the dictates of the dominating forces in Congress. . . .*[7]

Prepared for a fight, Johnson took his message directly to the people. In the upcoming November Congressional elections, the issue would be whether Congress would accept the president's policies and seat the southern congressmen. In a campaign called the "swing around the circle," Johnson traveled through more than twelve cities and towns, including Baltimore, Philadelphia, and New York City, seeking support. He blamed Congress for the unrest in the South, saying it was unwilling to restore the union.

Johnson's campaign was described as undignified. Fiery and argumentative, he quarreled with his audience and attacked those who disagreed with him. Du Bois wrote that Johnson practically caused a riot in Ohio.

> *At Cleveland his audience became a mob while the president himself increased the hubbub. The city authorities had made preparations for a polite reception, but as he proceeded with his harangue, the mob took complete possession of the crowd. Someone cried, "Why not hang Thad Stevens and Wendell Phillips?"*
>
> *"Yes," yelled Johnson "why not hang them?"*

In St. Louis Johnson blamed the New Orleans riot on Congress, citing the "diabolical and nefarious policies of Stevens, Phillips and Sumner." If Johnson hoped to gain support , he failed. In the election, the radicals gained a few seats in Congress, giving them enough strength to shape Reconstruction policy.[8]

When Johnson returned to Washington, he faced criticism. One politician described him as a "disgraced man, having gone out to win popular support, and having earned only public disgust." There was talk of impeachment, but Johnson did not back down.[9] When he addressed Congress, he chastised them for not seating the southern congressmen. Encouraged by the president's support, the Southerners refused to ratify the Fourteenth Amendment, even though their representatives would not be seated and their states could not rejoin the Union. When 1866 ended, Tennessee was the only southern state to have ratified the amendment.

The northern states did not rush to ratify it either. Blacks could vote only in five New England states, of which three—Maine, Vermont, and New Hampshire—had very few blacks. Connecticut and New Hampshire ratified the amendment a month after it was proposed, but other northern states opposed it. Most Republicans were moderate and viewed black suffrage as radical Republican madness. One Northerner said "it would make blacks the social and political equal of whites." Another "saw in it a desperate effort by the Republicans" to gain political power through the black vote.[10]

Political expediency, however, accomplished what the struggles of men and women who had fought a good fight against slavery and racism could not. In 1867 the northern states slowly, reluctantly, began to ratify the Fourteenth Amendment. They realized that reentering southern states would be entitled to at least twenty-nine Congressional seats. Most of the returning Southerners would be Democrats, the majority party in the South, and would align themselves with Democrats in the North. The Democratic Party would then hold the majority of the seats in Congress.

Unless they gave black men the vote, they would lose their hold as the majority party in Congress and would never be able to build a solid base in the South. As one congressman wrote, "The Republican or Union white men at the South were not sufficient in numbers to make their power or influence felt. The necessities of the situation, therefore, left no alternative but the enfranchisement of the blacks."[11]

Fourteenth Amendment (adopted 1868)

Section 1.
All persons born or naturalized in the United States, and subject to the jurisdiction thereof, are citizens of the United States and of the state wherein they reside. No state shall make or enforce any law which shall abridge the privileges or immunities of citizens of the United States; nor shall any state deprive any person of life, liberty, or property without due process of law; nor deny to any person within its jurisdiction the equal protection of the law.

Section 2.
Representatives shall be appportioned among the several states according to their respective numbers, counting the whole number of persons in each state. . . .

Section 3.
No person shall be a senator or representative in Congress, or elector of President and Vice President, or hold any office, civil or military, under the United States, or under any state, who having previously taken an oath, as a member of Congress, or as an officer of the United States, or as a member of any state legislature, or as an executive or judicial officer of any state, to support the Constitution of the United States, shall have engaged in insurrection or rebellion against the same, or given aid and comfort to the enemies thereof. But Congress may, by a vote of two-thirds of each House, remove such disability.

Section 4.
The validity of the public debt of the United States, authorized by law, including debts incurred for payment of pensions, and bounties for services in suppressing insurrection or rebellion, shall not be questioned. But neither the United States nor any state shall assume or pay any debt or obligation incurred in aid of insurrection or rebellion against the United States, or any claim for the loss or emanicpation of any slave; but all such debts, obligations, and claims shall be held illegal and void.

Section 5.
The Congress shall have power to enforce, by appropriate legislation, the provisions of this article.

Congress took the final steps to wrest control of Reconstruction from the president. It moved the traditional December convening of the first session nine months earlier—to March 1867. Congress seized this time to enact additional Reconstruction bills and prevent the president from implementing his policies. Congress also devised a plan to give black men suffrage in the South.

Beginning with the first Reconstruction Act of March 2, 1867, Congress instituted its plan. The former Confederate states were divided into five military districts:

I. Virginia
II. North and South Carolina
III. Georgia, Alabama, and Florida
IV. Mississippi and Arkansas
V. Louisiana and Texas

Each district would be commanded by an army general, with a force to keep the peace. The army commanders would supervise the election of delegates to the state conventions. The delegates would create new state constitutions. The most revolutionary aspect of the Reconstruction Act was that most adult males, regardless of color, would be allowed to vote for delegates to the constitutional conventions. The only people excluded, besides women, were men who had been active in the Confederate government. When the voters ratified the new state constitutions and the Thirteenth and Fourteenth Amendments, and Congress approved the state's new constitution, the state would be readmitted to the Union and its representatives accepted into Congress.[12]

Johnson, angry, vetoed the act, saying that it was unconstitutional and that it subjected the people of ten states to military law after they had already established order. He said that the freedmen "have not asked for the privilege of voting, and the vast majority of them have no idea of what it means."[13] His meeting with Frederick Douglass a year earlier had seemingly left no impression. Congress passed the Reconstruction Act over the president's veto, and then passed another bill, spelling out how the act would be implemented.

Even though these two bills were passed over presidential vetoes, the 1867 elections reflected growing northern dissatisfaction with the Republican

A cartoon of 1867 reveals the hostility among some whites to giving blacks the right to vote. The angry man at the left (who seems to resemble President Johnson) is also disdainful of the suffragist movement.

Party. Ohio voters rejected a black suffrage amendment by 38,000 votes and elected a Democratic legislature. Democrats also won in Connecticut, Pennsylvania, and New York. New Jersey did not change its voting regulations and continued to limit voting to white males. Maryland passed a law granting suffrage to white males only.

Adding to the bitterness of this period, in August, Johnson suspended his Secretary of War, Edwin M. Stanton, in violation of the Office of Tenure Act which Congress had passed earlier in the year. The bill prevented the president from dismissing members of his cabinet without the consent of the Senate. (The constitutionality of the act was questionable, and it was repealed when Johnson completed his term of office.) Congress began an impeachment investigation against the president. After Senate hearings in 1868, the vote was one short of the two-thirds majority needed to impeach a president.

However, Andrew Johnson's term of office was ending, and Congress had finally won the battle to control Reconstruction. Many people predicted dire consequences if freedmen gained the vote. They claimed that blacks were too ignorant and gullible to make wise decisions. Their votes would be controlled either by their old masters or by their "new masters," the Republicans. Johnson declared that it was evident that blacks were "utterly so ignorant of public affairs that their voting can consist in nothing more than carrying a ballot to the place where they are directed to deposit it."[14]

Would Andrew Johnson's prediction prove true? How would approximately 703,400 black men in the former Confederate states vote? Were they merely dupes of Republican carpetbaggers who were using them to retain power?[15] Would sharp politicians control their votes? How could people who were uneducated and had been enslaved participate in government? How could a people so dependent and inexperienced assume the responsibilities that came with freedom?

Perhaps, however, they were not as unprepared as some people supposed.

10. The New South

I believe my friends and fellow citizens, we are not prepared for this suffrage, but we can learn. Give a man tools and let him commence to use them, and in time he will learn a trade. So it is with voting. We may not understand it at the start, but in time we shall learn to do our duty.

William Beverly Nash
State Senator, South Carolina, 1868-1877

Even before the abolition of slavery, groups of black people—in the South and in the North, whether living in slavery or in the restricted range allowed "free blacks"—prepared for the time when they would become free citizens of the American nation. Wherever and however they could, men and women of African descent lay the foundations to support their freedom. African-American churches were among the earliest black institutions. All states with large slave populations, even northern states, had laws prohibiting enslaved people from congregating, except for work or sometimes for religious purposes. Thus, the church was not only a place to worship, but also a place to meet and, in many instances, a place to plan escapes.

Religious organizations were the heart of the black community in slavery and in freedom, whether the religious services were held in a shelter made of vines and branches during slavery, or in a church building. The church was a social, educational, political, charitable, and cultural outlet. In 1794, Richard Allen founded Bethel African Methodist Episcopal Church (A.M.E.) in Philadelphia, Pennsylvania, one of the first black denominations. Free black populations in Charleston, New Orleans, and other southern cities also established churches, schools, social organizations, and self-help societies before the war. Therefore, when slavery

Mother Bethel African Methodist Church in Philadelphia is often identified as the first church for blacks in the United States.

ended, there was a small cadre of blacks in every state ready to step into leadership roles.

Men such as John Mercer Langston were prepared for suffrage and for leadership. Langston was freeborn in Virginia, the son of a white planter and a freed black woman, possibly the planter's slave. Young John was five when his parents died in 1834; however, his father left an inheritance for his education. Langston attended Oberlin University in Ohio, one of the few colleges that accepted blacks and women. The town of Oberlin was an abolitionist stronghold before the Civil War. Langston was admitted to the Ohio bar in 1854 and became the first African-American allowed to practice law in Ohio.[1]

Langston was active in the abolitionist movement and became a respected leader during Reconstruction. He was an organizer of the National Equal Rights League, a black political and civil rights organization that was the forerunner of the National Association for the Advancement of Colored People (NAACP), one of the oldest civil rights organizations.

Forty-one delegates from ten states, including New York, New Jersey, and Pennsylvania, attended the league's first meeting in Cleveland, Ohio, in 1865. The delegates debated strategies for helping black people to overcome "invidious distinctions based on color."[2] One delegate requested that as the southern states were reconstructed, the "elective franchise be extended to men of color in those States. . . . That as colored men have fought to defend and perpetuate the unity of this Government, and maintain its liberties, every principle of honor demands that they should be placed on a footing with other citizens."[3]

The league's message to black Americans stressed "the necessity of acquiring property, of educating their children and themselves." The delegates also drew up a resolution calling for educated blacks to fill teaching positions. "In the present condition of the South it is imperatively necessary that the positions of teachers for our people in that section be filled by persons of our own color."[4]

League members opposed colonization and other emigration schemes. "Resolved, that we have no sympathy with any movement having for its object, the Colonizing of Colored Americans on the coast of Africa, or elsewhere." They applauded black missionaries spreading Christianity in Africa, but felt that talk of colonization diverted people's attention from the issue of enfranchisement.[5]

John Mercer Langston

John Mercer Langston was president of the National Equal Rights League until 1868. He helped organize league chapters in Maryland and Virginia, and in some western and northeastern states in an effort to build a strong political organization that could influence public officials and legislation.

In 1867, when Congress was working on the Reconstruction Acts, Langston and other league officers sponsored a convention in Washington, D.C. Approximately one hundred black men from seventeen states met to petition Congress, informing them of the "grievances and wants" of black people. Langston wrote that blacks were seeking "impartial justice, one that brings safety and peace to the loyal white American, happiness and prosperity to our common country, while it is the shield and buckler, the strong defense of the American freedmen."[6]

Other league members included Octavius V. Catto, principal of the black high school in Philadelphia, who was active in the struggle for equal rights in that city. He was killed in 1871 by whites when he tried to exercise his right to vote. Peter H. Clark, another league member, was the principal of a black high school in Cincinnati, Ohio. Clark had been a "conductor" on the underground railroad, leading runaway slaves through Ohio into Canada. Some league members had been slaves. Jermain W. Loguen escaped slavery and worked as a porter while attending night school, and became active in the abolitionist movement. He also became a bishop in the African Methodist Episcopal Zion Church. John S. Rock was born into a free black New Jersey family in 1825. He was one of the "outstanding leaders in the movement for equal rights for black Americans in the North." Rock, a brilliant man, taught school, and then studied and practiced dentistry, medicine, and law. In 1865 Rock was sworn in as the first African-American to be accredited to argue cases before the Supreme Court.[7]

Other sources of political education for the new voters were the black veterans of the Union army. These men, many of them former slaves, came home from the war prepared to vote and take on the responsibilities of free men. Many joined the Union League, which was started by patriotic northern Republicans to support the war effort. Southern chapters were organized by loyal southern whites—Unionists—for the same purpose. After the war, league chapters in the South became a political training ground for the freedmen.

Electioneering in the South, as shown in an engraving from Harper's Weekly, *July 25, 1868.*

Most of these local chapters were segregated, although in some blacks and whites cooperated and worked well together.[8] Meetings were held in black schools and churches and sometimes in members' homes. Because of the threat of violence, these gatherings were held secretly.

At the meetings, Republican newspapers were read aloud by a literate member—a black veteran who had learned to read in the army, a teacher, a minister, or anyone else who could help other members understand the voting process, the rights of citizens, and the political and social issues of the time. Thomas Allen, a former slave who organized a league chapter in Georgia, was a "Baptist preacher, shoemaker, and farmer." His ability to read made him an important member of his community, and in 1868 he was elected to the Georgia legislature. "In my county the colored people came to me for instructions, and I gave them the best instructions I could. I took the *New York Tribune* and other papers, and in that way I found out a great deal, and I told them whatever I thought was right."[9] Henry Holt was a freedman active in a North Carolina chapter. Holt, who could neither read nor write, said, "We just went there. . . . we talked a little; made speeches on one question and another."[10]

A new world opened for these men as they took part in political discussions. League meetings served other functions, too. The chapters offered protection to freedmen making tentative steps into the political arena. Armed guards, many of them veterans of the Union black regiments, guarded league meetings and trained the freedmen in self-defense. In one South Carolina county, a group of Union League freedman forced a local judge to arrest a white man who had assaulted a black man. A group of Alabama sharecroppers sought guidance from the organization as they tried to get fair treatment from landowners.

Many former Confederates, however, complained that the Union League was merely a way to control the black vote and put dangerous ideas of social equality in their heads. It was, they said, another Republican trick.

The years 1867 to 1869 saw a whirlwind of political activity in the former Confederate states, as Congressional Reconstruction was established. Registration of qualified voters was the first step in forming the new governments. Voters elected delegates to rewrite the state constitutions, creating laws that would transform the South. The work of organizing the elections fell to the army generals in command of the five military districts. Not only was most of the black electorate voting for the first time, and unable to read or write, but a sizable portion of the whites were also first-time voters and, according to one historian, 35 percent of them were illiterate as well.[11]

Some whites had never voted before because of local property or literacy requirements. Before the war, wealthy slaveholding planters and merchants had a stranglehold on local and state governments. As Andrew Johnson had suggested, the end of slavery brought freedom to the poor white population, too; few of whom had ever participated in the political process.

The Reconstruction Acts created a new electorate in the South. Men who had remained loyal to the federal government during the war, who had no

African-Americans voting in 1867

criminal record, and who had lived in the state for at least a year were allowed to vote. The majority of the people who met these qualifications were blacks whose loyalty to the federal government was unquestioned; and Northerners who had relocated to the South and met residency requirements.

More than one million people qualified to participate in the electoral process in the former Confederate states—approximately 660,000 whites and 703,400 blacks.[12]

The voters elected more than 1,000 delegates to attend the constitutional conventions. The majority of the delegates were Republicans. One-sixth of the white delegates were Union army veterans who had settled in the South. A number were professionals—lawyers, doctors, and businessmen. Most of the white delegates, however, were Unionist Southerners. Some had fought in the Union army; others had been imprisoned for activities supporting the Union. They were primarily from the "upcountry" regions of Alabama, Georgia, North Carolina, and Tennessee, and were farmers, small-business owners, artisans, and, in some cases, professionals.[13]

DELEGATES TO THE STATE CONSTITUTIONAL CONVENTIONS 1867-1868

State	Black Delegates	White Delegates
Alabama	18	90
Arkansas	8	58
Florida	18	28
Georgia	33	137
Louisiana	17	83
Mississippi	17	83
North Carolina	15	118
South Carolina	76	48
Texas	9	81
Virginia	25	80

Data from: Reconstruction After the Civil War. *2nd edition. John Hope Franklin.*

While 265 of the delegates were African-American, they were the majority only in the Louisiana and South Carolina conventions. Some black delegates would gain elective offices once the states were readmitted to the Union and elections were held for state representatives. Most of the black delegates were ministers; others were skilled workers—carpenters, blacksmiths, and barbers. There were some teachers, a few farmers, and a very few field hands. Northerners who had relocated to the South accounted for 28, and 40 were veterans who had served in the Union army's black regiments.[14]

Although the delegates were overwhelmingly Republican, the differences in their backgrounds and experiences caused dissension. Gaining equal rights with other citizens and equal justice under the law, public schools, freedom of movement, and land ownership were crucial issues for the black delegates and the people who voted them in. A group of delegates in the Alabama convention expressed the views of many freedmen:

> *We claim exactly the same rights, privileges, and immunities as are enjoyed by white men—we ask nothing more and will be content with nothing less. . . . The law no longer knows white nor black, but simply men, and consequently we are entitled to ride in public conveyances, hold office, sit on juries, and do everything else which we have in the past been prevented from doing solely on the ground of color.[15]*

The delegates of both races agreed to eliminate laws that allowed whipping, debtors' prisons, and property requirements to sit on juries and to vote. Other issues were more difficult.[16] "Carpetbagging" delegates from the North favored economic growth, such as railroad development and establishment of industrial enterprises.[17] Southern delegates, especially those from upcountry regions, wanted to bar the southern aristocracy from holding office and regaining control over local communities.

In some state conventions, the more conservative white southern delegates opposed using tax funds to support schools, especially schools for black children. Most delegations agreed to a public school system, but would not clearly state whether white children and black children should attend school together. Only in South Carolina and Louisiana, where the majority of the delegates were black, did laws specifically state that schools should be integrated. These delegates

The fight to gain the right to sit on juries was long and bitter. Here an artist of the period shows a racially mixed jury in a southern courtroom in 1867.

feared that otherwise, black schools would not receive a fair share of school funds. The South Carolina law read that "all public schools, colleges, and universities of this state, supported in whole or in part by the public funds, shall be free and open to all the children and youths of this state without regard to race or color."[18]

The question of social equality divided the delegates. Conservative white delegates resisted legislation encouraging social equality, claiming they wanted their state constitutions to appeal to the general population. Black delegates attempted to pass laws allowing people of African descent to stay in hotels, eat in restaurants, and use public transportation. Many delegates knew the inconvenience and humiliation of being refused admission to hotels and restaurants, and denied first-class accommodations on public conveyances. After lengthy debate, the issue of access to public accommodations was still not directly addressed. Only Louisiana enacted a law that specifically said that access to public transportation facilities and businesses licensed by the state could not be denied to an individual because of race.[19]

However, most white Southerners resented the Reconstruction process and considered the constitutions illegitimate documents that did not represent them, their values, or their culture. They believed the federal government was punishing them. They saw the military as an occupying force, kept in the South for the purpose of crushing southern whites and imposing northern Republican rule.

When the new constitution in South Carolina was ratified, it was called the "work of sixty-odd Negroes, many of them ignorant and depraved, together with fifty white men, outcasts of northern society, and southern renegades, betrayers of their race and country." The North Carolina delegates—118 whites and 15 blacks—were called mules and jackasses. Louisiana's new constitution was denigrated as the "work of the lowest and most corrupt body of men ever assembled in the South. It was the work of ignorant Negroes cooperating with a gang of white adventurers, strangers to our interests and our sentiments."[20]

The attacks were harsh and exaggerated, and did not fairly analyze the new constitutions. It was clear that the former Confederates would not quietly accept new leadership. In protest, many southern white voters stayed away from the polls, refusing to ratify the constitutions. Congress quickly enacted a new law in 1868, basing ratification on the number of people who actually voted, rather than on the number of eligible voters.

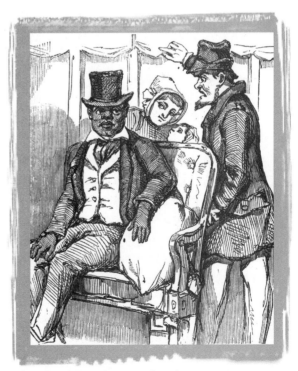

Jim Crow laws being enforced on a train

By the spring of 1868, the constitutions of nine former Confederate states had been ratified. The exceptions were Mississippi and Alabama. These new constitutions erased the Black Codes, guaranteed equal rights for all citizens, made school attendance compulsory, and created the first public school system in the South. Laws were also enacted providing for the use of public funds to support orphanages, hospitals, and institutions for the mentally ill and physically impaired. In the past, public funds had rarely been used to support social programs. Each state's constitution had to provide for universal suffrage—giving all male citizens twenty-one or older the right to vote—and ratification of the Thirteenth and Fourteenth Amendments. Without these last provisions, Congress would not approve the constitution.

As the former Confederate states rejoined the Union, it appeared as if the Republicans were on their way to creating a new South. However, many Southerners wanted their old South back. Hatred and resentment ran as deep as the rivers and streams. A Democratic newspaper in Charleston, South Carolina, in 1868, predicted that the new constitutions would last only as long as the military remained in the South.[21]

The 1868 presidential election would determine whether the Republicans could retain their hold on the former Confederate states. They chose Ulysses S. Grant to run for president, against Democrat Horatio Seymour, governor of New York State—a "copperhead" Northerner who supported the South during the Civil War. If Seymour and the Democrats won, the reforms of congressional Reconstruction might be repealed. Because of the new black voters, the Republicans were confident of victory in the South; however, their traditional northern base seemed to be eroding, and Democrats were winning more seats in the North and the West.

Violence and intimidation were used to keep blacks from voting and participating in politics. Black workers were threatened with job loss if they took out time to vote. In southwest Georgia, a mob of 400 whites attacked a group of blacks holding an election day parade. In Louisiana, Republican meetings were interrupted by white attackers, a Republican newspaper office was destroyed, and nearly 200 blacks were killed in other incidents. The military commander in the area did nothing to stop the violence and advised blacks not to vote.[22] Violence was an ever-present threat that eventually weakened and destroyed the Union League chapters in the South.

When Ulysses S. Grant won the election, it appeared that the Republicans were still in power and Reconstruction would proceed as outlined by Congress. However, the effects of violence and intimidation were clearly seen in the Georgia and Louisiana presidential races where Horatio Seymour was the winner. This was only the beginning. Southerners had been defeated in the war, but they remained determined not to keep the peace until the army and the carpetbaggers were gone and blacks were returned to the plantations, as landless laborers with few civil or political rights.

Yet some of the freed men and women had hopes of a new day in a new South. Once the state constitutions were ratified and the former Confederate states were allowed to return to the Union, elections were held to vote for new representatives. Some newly elected leaders were men of African descent.

The first African-Americans to serve in Congress: (Top, standing, left to right) Robert C. De Large of South Carolina, Jefferson H. Long of Georgia. (Seated, left to right) H. R. Revels of Mississippi, Benjamin S. Turner of Alabama, Josiah T. Walls of Florida, Joseph N. Raincy of South Carolina, and R. Brown Elliot of South Carolina. Revels was a senator; the others were representatives.

II. Men of the People

The spirit of our people must be aroused.
They must feel and act as men.
John Mercer Langston

The black men who held office during Reconstruction were neither ignorant nor illiterate—although this stereotype persisted well into the twentieth century. They were not thoroughly manipulated by wicked carpetbaggers from the North who came to the South to take economic advantage of the downtrodden white Southerner. Nor were they dupes of the scalawags—native white Southerners who cooperated with the Republicans in bringing corruption and suffering to the people of the South. However, the image of ignorant former slaves fresh from the cotton fields, tarnishing the halls of southern legislatures, was prevalent. Who, then, were the black men who took office three years after slavery had ended?

Many had participated in the state conventions of 1867 and 1868. Most had been born in the South and were literate. The historian Eric Foner, in *Freedom's Lawmakers: A Directory of Black Officeholders During Reconstruction*, has identified 1,510 black men who held office during Reconstruction. Of this number, 387 had been slaves, 327 were freeborn, 54 had been enslaved and later freed. It is unknown whether the remaining men were slave or free before the war.[1]

Of the black officeholders, 962 were literate, 201 were illiterate, and the educational status of the remaining 347 is unknown. The majority of the black leaders in South Carolina and Louisiana came from the educated free black population of Charleston and New Orleans, where free blacks had established private schools or hired tutors for their children.

The black councilmen elected in Raleigh, North Carolina, were all literate. Even during slavery, North Carolina was more liberal than other slave

A woodcut of the Reconstruction period shows "The African Race in Congress—Hon. John Willis Menard Addressing the House of Representatives, Washington, D.C., February 27th, 1869."

states and allowed some education for blacks. Educational and religious training was provided by the Quakers, Presbyterians, and other denominations, which probably accounts for the high rate of literacy among the Raleigh councilmen.[2] In other states, a few blacks secretly learned the rudiments of reading and writing from literate slaves. Occasionally, an enslaved child was taught with the slaveholder's children. And some black Reconstruction lawmakers had been born and educated in the North.

The African-American Reconstruction leaders were similar to other Americans in their philosophies, ideals, and beliefs. Whether they had been slave or free, they were, after all, "made in America" and shared the same democratic principles of other Americans. Many, like Holland Thompson, were local leaders.

Thompson, born in 1830 in Montgomery, Alabama, was a "physically impressive" man; six feet tall, and handsome. He was "a young, ambitious, and able former slave who was a fine orator." Thompson had been hired out by his master, William Taylor, to work as a waiter in a Montgomery hotel, which may have been where he learned to read and write. Thompson remained enslaved until the war ended and then opened a grocery store that became a leading black business in Montgomery. He also helped found the First Colored Baptist Church of Montgomery and organize the Baptist State Convention.

In 1868, Thompson was elected to the city council from the fifth ward, which was 55 percent black. Like most black Reconstructionists, he tried to help fellow blacks. He staunchly fought for civil and political rights for the freedmen. Because of his efforts, laws were passed during his time in office that gave equal pay to blacks and whites working as street cleaners. He helped to bring a branch of the Freedmen's Bank to Montgomery, and he fought for fairer taxation laws. He was a man of his people, with a strong following in his ward. His leadership was crucial in helping his fellow freedmen through this difficult yet hopeful period.[3]

Robert Smalls was one of the most famous Reconstruction leaders. Born into slavery in Beaufort, South Carolina, he was hired out as a boy to work in Charleston where he learned the art of navigation. In a celebrated escape, Smalls, employed by the Confederacy as a pilot on the ship the *Planter*, sailed out of Charleston Harbor and delivered the *Planter*, with his family on board, to the Union navy in 1862.

After the war, Smalls became a successful businessman in Beaufort and hired tutors to learn to read and write. He began his political career in 1868, representing Beaufort County in the constitu-

Robert Smalls

tional convention. As a delegate, he advocated compulsory school attendance for all children. He supported schools and education throughout his long political career.

Smalls was elected to the state house of representatives in 1868. He then served in the state senate from 1870 to 1875. He won election in 1875 to the U.S. House of Representatives and held that office for a total of five terms: 1875-79; 1882-83 (serving after a contested election); 1884-85 (filling a vacancy); and 1885-87.[4]

Francis Cardozo was freeborn in 1837 in Charleston, South Carolina. His father was described by Eric Foner as the "prominent Jewish businessman and economist Isaac N. Cardozo," and his mother was a free woman of mixed black and Native American ancestry. Cardozo attended a private school for free blacks in Charleston.[5]

Since opportunities for a higher education were limited because of his race, his father sent him to Scotland to attend the University of Glasgow. After graduation, he attended Presbyterian seminaries in Edinburgh and London. In 1864, Cardozo returned to the United States and was ordained as a Congregationalist minister in New Haven, Connecticut. He then went to Charleston in 1865 to minister to the freedmen. He helped to establish the Avery Normal Institute, a school in Charleston, South Carolina.

Educational development remained at the center of Cardozo's activities as he became involved in state government. He was chairman of the educational committee of the state constitutional convention of 1868 and helped develop a public school system in South Carolina. In 1872 he was elected state treasurer, and helped reorganize the South Carolina Land Commission, correcting its serious management and corruption problems.

Robert Brown Elliott was one of the most militant and outspoken of the Reconstruction leaders. He was "deep-chested, broad shouldered with abundant hair."[6] Elliott was a skillful lawyer and an eloquent speaker. In 1874 he held the House of Representatives spellbound with an impassioned speech in support of Charles Sumner's Civil Rights Bill. "The Constitution warrants it: The Supreme Court sanctions it; justice demands it," Elliott declared.

Recent scholarship suggests he was born in Liverpool, England, where he attended school. Elliott was well educated and a typesetter by trade. He possibly came to Boston on a British naval vessel around 1866. He worked as a type-setter in Boston and then found his way to Charleston, where he became associate editor of the South Carolina *Leader*, a Republican newspaper. His political career began when he became a delegate to the constitutional convention of 1868 in South Carolina and his rise was then meteoric. He was nominated for lieutenant governor at the Republican convention of 1868 but dropped out after finishing third on the first ballot. He then won election to the South Carolina House of Representatives when he was twenty-six. He was elected to the U.S. House of Representatives in 1870 and reelected two years later but resigned in 1874 and returned to South Carolina to "fight political corruption."[7]

Elliot was appointed chairman of the Committee on Railroads and was the only black on the five-person Board of Commissioners. He was also appointed to the Committee on Privileges and Elections and served as assistant adjutant general, founded a state militia, and was speaker of the state House of Representatives from 1874 to 1876.

Robert Brown Elliott

Elliott supported legislation to help both blacks and whites. He fought a poll tax and a literacy test for voters, recognizing that these could subvert black voting rights. He also fought for the cancellation of debts, which helped white planters who had lost their property during the war. He supported federal laws to stop the Ku Klux Klan and voted against a bill to pardon rebels.[8] He supported the integration of hotels, restaurants, and transportation.

These are but a few of the people who provided leadership during the Reconstruction period. Sixteen black men served in Congress; eighteen held major state offices, and more than 500 other blacks held seats in their state legislatures. There was, however, no "Negro domination" of these legislative bodies, as many Southerners claimed. In Texas, out of 100 lawmakers in its legislature, 14 were black. In the North Carolina General Assembly, there were 21 blacks; and in the Georgia legislature, 32 (out of 216). Even in Mississippi, Alabama, and Louisiana, where larger numbers of blacks held state legislative office, whites controlled the important committees, and few of the bills introduced by black lawmakers were passed.

African-American legislators were in the majority in the South Carolina House of Representatives, and by 1873 had a majority in the state senate as well.[9] Black lawmakers such as Robert Brown Elliott sat on key committees and were able to push through important bills. South Carolina was the only state that made any movement toward land distribution, creating the South Carolina Land Commission that enabled 14,000 black families and some white families as well to purchase land under favorable credit terms.[10]

In plantation counties where blacks were in the majority, they held positions such as sheriff, county supervisor, tax collector, school board member, election commissioner, and justice of the peace. Blacks sat on city and town councils, and a few towns even had a black mayor [11]

The black Reconstruction leaders had only as much power as their white Republican suppporters gave them, and were not as imperfect as they have been historically portrayed. Some—such as Robert Elliot—were brilliant and talented. Others were mediocre and too easily controlled and influenced by whites—sometimes to the point of corruption. Some were self-serving and some worked tirelessly for their constituency. Some were barely literate, while others had university educations. Some were too conservative and would not or could not respond to the freedmen's passion for land. Others loved their political appointments and elective offices too much and made too many compromises to keep them.

It was in the area of education that the Reconstruction leaders had the greatest impact. The southern Reconstruction legislatures established, for the first time, a public school system in the South—a region that had historically resisted using public funds to support schools for all youngsters, rich or poor, black and white. This was one of the abiding legacies of the Reconstruction era.

Brief Biography
JOHN R. LYNCH

John R. Lynch

In December 1873, when John Roy Lynch took his congressional seat, he was only twenty-six—the youngest member of the Forty-third Congress. Lynch also was one of the few black Reconstruction leaders to leave a written account of this era. In 1913 he wrote *The Facts of Reconstruction*, and in 1938, at the age of ninety-one, he completed *Reminiscences of an Active Life: the Autobiography of John R. Lynch*. The autobiography, however, was not published until 1970, long after Lynch's death. These books give us a firsthand look at Reconstruction from the point of view of a black person who had been enslaved and emancipated before actively participating in Reconstruction politics. Lynch's books also refute the standard picture of Reconstruction—as a time when ignorant ex-slaves and greedy Northerners oppressed the defeated South.

When *The Facts of Reconstruction* was published it did not receive much notice; however, the historian James M. McPherson wrote in the book's introduction that it "stands up well in the light of modern scholarship and must be regarded as an important landmark in the historiography [historical writing] of Reconstruction." In his preface, John R. Lynch describes himself as "one of the few remaining links in the chain by which the present generation is connected with the Reconstruction period—the most important and eventful period in our country's history." Lynch was at the center of that "eventful period" as observer and participant.

John Roy Lynch was born on September 10, 1847, on a plantation in Concordia Parish, Louisiana. His father, Patrick Lynch, was born in Dublin and brought to the United States as a boy with his family. Lynch's mother, Catherine White, was a house slave on the plantation where Patrick Lynch was manager. John Lynch says in his autobiography that his father "soon found himself a victim to her commanding presence, her charming and captivating beauty, her perfect form and winning ways. . . ."[1] The couple fell in love, and Catherine bore him three children; however, Catherine was still a slave. Since a slave could not enter into a contract, their marriage was not legal. Her relationship with Patrick was conducted with the consent of her owner. She and the three children she bore were the property of the plantation owner. Patrick Lynch, therefore, made arrangements to buy Catherine and their children so that they would become his property. He could then free them and legally marry Catherine.

Unfortunately, Patrick became ill before the arrangements were completed. Knowing he was dying, he asked a friend to look after Catherine and his children and complete the arrangements so that they would be freed. But after Patrick died, the friend broke his promise, and Catherine and her children remained enslaved. When a new planter purchased the plantation, he removed Catherine and her children to Natchez, Mississippi. John R. Lynch and his mother and siblings were not freed until Yankee soldiers captured Natchez in 1863. John Lynch was only sixteen, and was at the starting point of a remarkable career.

"The problem of making a living was the one that was before me," John Lynch wrote in his autobiography. "I was without means and without an education. The only capital I possessed was youth, health, and a determination to win the race of life." And win the race of life he did.

He found work as a pantryman, managing the food supply of a Union regiment in Natchez. After the regiment left the city, he worked in a photography studio and attended a night school for black students, operated by northern teachers. After four months in 1866, the school was closed down because of violence against northern teachers. With this start, Lynch began the task of educating himself:

I had my books at my place of business. It frequently happened that I had time enough to devote two and, some days, as many as three hours to private study during the course of the day. Among the books that I carefully read and studied was one on parliamentary law, which I found to be of great advantage. . . . I also received, in an indirect way, some valuable assistance from the white public school. My place of business was in Main Street. The white public school was across the alley. I could easily hear the recitations that were going on in the school across the way. I would sometimes sit in the back room for hours and listen with close attention. . . . I could clearly and distinctly hear the questions asked by the teacher and the responses given by the class. . . . I could also see and read the problems in arithmetic that were on the blackboard. . . . The knowledge and information thus obtained proved to be of great assistance to me.[2]

Lynch became interested in Republican Reconstruction politics during these politically charged times. He joined a political club, where his natural talents and intelligence gained him attention as he wrote and spoke of Mississippi's new state constitution.

In 1869 General Adelbert Ames, the Republican military governor, appointed Lynch justice of the peace in Natchez. It was the first time a black person had been appointed to a civil office in Mississippi. Lynch also won a seat on the state legislature that year, and became speaker of the house and a leading voice in state government. He was still in his early twenties.

In 1873 Lynch won election to the House of Representatives. He was instrumental in the passage of the Civil Rights Bill in 1875. One historian wrote that Lynch "had more influence at the White House than any other black man until modern times."[3] Lynch was re-elected to congress from Mississippi three times, serving until 1877 and once again in 1882 to 1883.

Lynch enjoyed a long and varied career. In 1896 he was admitted to the bar in Mississippi and Washington, D.C. He owned a plantation in Mississippi, joined the army during the Spanish-American War, and retired as a major. After the war he moved to Chicago and practiced law. John Roy Lynch died in 1939 at the age of ninety-two.

12. Educating the Freedmen

I recall that I looked forward with an anxious appetite to the "teacher's day" at our little cabin.

Booker T. Washington

A system of public education was one of the most important and enduring accomplishments of the Reconstruction era. Traditionally, southern communities had been reluctant to pay taxes for the support of public institutions, including schools. The plantation owners dominated local and state governments, controlling taxation and the ways in which public money would be used. These wealthy planters and slave owners had private schools and tutors for their children.

White children from poor families received little schooling. Sometimes they learned a trade from their father or were apprenticed to a skilled worker. Enslaved black children received no schooling and, in many states, laws prohibited teaching them to read and write. Yet, in spite of the risk involved, there were secret black schools in the South and brave teachers to run them. Susie King Taylor, a black nurse and teacher, described in her memoirs the difficulties of attaining an education:

> *I was born under the slave law in Georgia in 1848 and was brought up by my grandmother in Savannah. . . . We were sent to a friend of my grandmother, a Mrs. Woodhouse, a widow, to learn to read and write. She was a free woman. . . . We went every day with our books wrapped in paper to prevent the police or white persons from seeing them. We went in, one at a time, through the gate into the yard to the kitchen, which was the school room. She had 25 or 30 children whom she taught, assisted by her daughter, Mary Jane. The neighbors. . . supposed we were there learning trades, as it was the custom to give children a trade of some kind.[1]*

Susie King Taylor, in a photo printed in her book, Reminiscences of My Life in Camp.

Susie King Taylor continued her education and became a nurse and a teacher for a black Civil War regiment, teaching many of the soldiers—most of them fresh out of slavery—to read and write.

Education, along with the wish for land, were important goals of the freed men and women. Du Bois described this wish:

They were consumed with the desire for schools. . . . The movement that was started was irresistible. It planted the free common school in a part of the nation. . .where it had never been known, and never been recognized before. Free, then, with a desire for land and a frenzy for schools, the Negro lurched into the new day.[2]

One of the first freedmen's schools to be sponsored by a northern organization opened in Fortress Monroe, Virginia, in September 1861, and served the children of the black refugees who had fled to the fort. The school began with six students and grew to fifty or sixty by the end of September. Classes were conducted by Mary Peake, a free black woman. The school was sponsored by the American Missionary Association (AMA) and classes were held in the teacher's small house. Mrs. Peake and the AMA believed that day school should prepare the student for Sunday or Sabbath school; therefore, prayers and hymns were an important part of the curriculum.

In 1861 and 1862 freedmen's schools, aided by the government, were opened in southeastern Virginia in Hampton, Norfolk, Newport News, Yorktown, Mill Creek, and Portsmouth.[3] Freedmen's schools were also established in the early years of the war in the coastal regions of South

A freedmen's school in the South in 1870

Carolina. After Union troops occupied the Sea Islands in 1861 and 1862, General Sherman issued a message to the people of the North, calling for teachers to instruct the freedmen.

> *The helpless condition of the blacks inhabiting the vast area in the occupation of this command calls for immediate action on the part of a highly favored and philanthropic people. . . . until the blacks become capable of themselves of thinking and acting judiciously, the services of competent instructors will be received. . . . Never was there a nobler or more fitting opportunity for the operation of that considerate and practical benevolence for which the northern people have ever been distinguished.*[4]

The AMA heard the general's call. Normally the association concentrated on religious matters, but it began mission work for the freed population. Teachers and missionaries were sent to Port Royal and the Sea Islands, where the newly emancipated slaves were organized on abandoned plantations.

Other groups, too, worked to save the minds and souls of the former slaves. Associations were formed in New York, Cincinnati, Philadelphia, and Boston. The Boston Educational Commission, the National Freedmen's Relief Association, and the Pennsylvania Relief Association were among many aid societies helping the freedmen. The Quakers organized schools and educational programs. Some societies felt that education was a secular, non-religious function of their organization; others required their teachers to be members of the church and to spread Christian teachings.

The work of the aid societies was of immeasurable value to these men and women and children, who for the first time had the opportunity to gain an education. However, when they were able to, black men and women worked to help themselves. On St. Helena Island, two freedmen taught approximately 150 students until additional teachers came from the North. Black organizations—especially churches—and educated black Northerners took active roles in educating and aiding the freedmen. The African Methodist Episcopal Church focused on aiding the former slaves. The African Civilization Society was established in Brooklyn, New York, in 1858 to train black missionaries to work in Africa. Society members described it as "an organization of pious and educated Colored people. . .who believe, and always have believed that the black man of education can best instruct, direct, and elevate his race."[5] The organization had been active in the antislavery movement and its leaders felt that black teachers better understood and were best suited to teach and understand black children. The society established schools in the District of Columbia, Virginia, and Maryland, and later in the Carolinas, Georgia, Mississippi, and Louisiana.[6]

The Freedmen's Bureau was at the center of the efforts to educate the freedmen. It provided services to the missionary societies and relief organizations that came south to educate the freedmen. The bureau allowed schools to be opened in unused government buildings and furnished transportation, books, supplies, and classrooms. The bureau also provided teachers with rations and living quarters.[7]

Laura M. Towne was one of the white volunteers who taught in freedmen's schools. This 1866 photo shows her with students in the South Carolina Sea Islands.

Booker T. Washington, an important black leader of the period, preached hard work and perseverance and built Tuskegee into a leading educational institution.

Fortunately, Commissioner Howard, head of the Freedmen's Bureau, was a staunch supporter of educational programs and believed that education would help the freed men and women and their children to assimilate into American culture and life. The growth of the schools, however, was the result of the determination of the freedmen and their dedicated teachers. Some families chose to work on plantations where their children were allowed to attend school, or where the planter had built a school. In some regions the freed people raised taxes among themselves to open schools. And in the Mississippi Valley, black families paid a monthly tuition rate of anywhere from twenty-five cents to a dollar and a quarter per student so that their schools were self-supporting.[8] It seemed to the black educator Booker T. Washington that a whole race was going to school.

Few people who were not right in the midst of the scene can form any exact idea of the intense desire which the people of my race showed for an education. . . . Few were too young, and none too old, to make the attempt to learn. As fast as any kind of teachers could be secured, not only were day-schools filled, but night-schools as well. The great ambition of the older people was to try to learn to read the Bible before they died . . . men and women who were fifty or seventy-five years old would often be found in the night-school. . . . the principal book studied in the Sunday-school was the spelling-book. Day-school, night-school, Sunday-school, were always crowded, and often many had to be turned away for want of room.[9]

13. John Brown's Body

We taught . . . the children "John Brown" which they entered into eagerly. I felt to the full the significance of that song being sung here in South Carolina by little [N]egro children, by those whom he—the glorious old man—died to save.

Charlotte Forten
Teacher

The story of Reconstruction after the Civil War appears to be a man's tale. We speak of the freedmen, meaning of course men and women. We speak of blacks winning the right to vote, and we mean black men because no woman, black or white, had the franchise. When we discuss black Reconstruction leaders, we speak the names of men only. Women appear to be silent and invisible.

However, without the women, the work of the men could not have been accomplished. In 1865, some black women left the cotton or rice fields to create homes for their children and husbands. Others remained in the fields, along with their mates, so that the family could survive. Black women and white women worked for the anti-slavery cause, and helped the

"Yankee schoolmarms" made an important contribution to the education of the freedmen.

117

freedmen and women once slavery ended: Harriet Tubman, Sojourner Truth, Frances Ellen Harper, Lydia Maria Child, and many others. It was the women, many whose names are unknown or forgotten, who helped to implement Reconstruction's lasting monument—a public school system.

The records of John W. Alvord, chief inspector of schools and finances for the Freedmen's Bureau, indicate that from 65 to 85 percent of the teachers during the early years of Reconstruction were female. Many were unmarried white women from the North—the "Yankee schoolmarms" who were an important part of the movement to educate the freedmen. They were expected to be skilled teachers, to exemplify high moral and religious values, and to be committed to their students.[1]

Black women from the North and from the South were also among the dedicated teachers. As more freedmen received an education, the population of black teachers grew. John Alvord's records reflect this growth. In January, 1867, approximately 1,092 white teachers and 549 black teachers were teaching in freedmen's schools. By 1870, there were 1,764 black teachers and 1,536 white teachers.[2] As early as 1867, one-third of the teachers in the freedmen's schools were black. Some of the best black schools were in New Orleans and Charleston. Because both these cities had large, free-black educated populations during slavery, there was a pool of competent blacks.[3] One freedmen's school in New Orleans served 300 students and was staffed and supported entirely by blacks.[4] In Charleston, Francis Cardozo was the superintendent of the American Missionary Association freedmen's schools. He set high standards and instituted stringent requirements for the teachers.

The black instructors in the freedmen's schools had varied personal histories. Harriet Jacobs was born into slavery and held in bondage for thirty years. She described this life in *Incidents in the Life of a Slave Girl*. Jacobs and her daughter ran a freedmen's school in Alexandria, Virginia. William and Ellen Craft, a couple who had escaped from slavery by disguising themselves as a master and slave traveling together, ran a vocational school in Georgia that had been founded by Boston abolitionists.

A number of the black teachers were well-educated freeborn men and women, including John Mercer Langston, Charlotte Forten, and Francis Cardozo. A few southern whites taught in freedmen's schools. Thomas B. Chaplin, a former plantation owner on St. Helena Island who had lost his property and money after the war, taught in a freedmen's school in 1872. However, his need for a regular salary may have been his motive, rather than a desire to educate former slaves.

After the war, freedmen's schools spread from the Virginia peninsula and the coastal regions of South Carolina to other parts of the South. These later freedmen's schools were bitterly resented by many Southerners and their anger was often directed at the northern teachers. One young white teacher in a Louisiana parish spent a whole day in the blistering heat trudging from house to house in the rural area where she had been hired, looking for a room. Every door in every home was closed to her. Some whites refused to rent to her because she taught in a freedmen's school; others refused because they feared their neighbors' anger. The teacher could not stay with a black family because of southern custom—blacks and whites did not mingle on a social level. A host family's house would most likely be burned. The problem of finding lodging became so serious in Louisiana that when General Banks was

At a hearing before the Senate Committee for the Investigation of Southern Outrages, a teacher from New York describes his experience of being "run out" of a southern town.

organizing Union-occupied territory, he said that he would pull the laborers off plantations if families in the region refused to rent rooms to teachers.[5]

Finding lodging was not the only problem in rural Louisiana parishes. One teacher complained that she had only "strong pork and sour bread" to eat—the food was probably spoiled. She was called a "nigger teacher" because she instructed black children. "Can't buy anything on credit," she said, "and haven't a cent of money. The school shed has no floor, and the rains sweep clean across it through the places where the windows should be."[6] Another teacher complained about a Union army officer who let his dogs roam free in the evenings so that the adults coming to school would be bitten.[7] Guards were called in to protect adults going to night school in another Louisiana parish after rocks were thrown at them. In North Carolina, too, teachers and school officials were threatened, sometimes receiving frightening letters.[8]

One reason for hostility toward the freedmen's schools was that planters thought they interfered with the labor force. On many plantations, young people worked in the fields either before or after classes. And during some portion of the planting and harvesting cycle, school was disbanded altogether.

In the years following the war, the number of black teachers increased, as at the "Zion School for Colored Children" in Charleston, South Carolina.

120

The main reason, however, for the anger against schools, and the northern teachers, was that Southerners believed the schools were breeding grounds for black troublemakers. They claimed the schools fostered ideas of social equality and were platforms for Republican propaganda.[9] Yet, the lessons and curriculum were, for the most part, not threatening. The aim of the freedmen's schools was to give the former slaves basic literacy and industrial training so they could be useful workers, productive citizens, and intelligent voters.

The writer and abolitionist Lydia Maria Child wrote an early textbook for freedmen. She included biographies of Frederick Douglass and other black heroes to inspire them. She also presented poems, essays, and anecdotes on health, morality, and raising children, since there were many adult students in night schools. Loyalty to God and country, the importance of work, and the need to forgive, were common themes in the instructional material.

In her diary, the teacher and writer Charlotte Forten (later Charlotte Forten Grimke) described her experiences teaching on St. Helena Island, in South Carolina: "We went into the school, and heard the children read and spell. The teachers tell us that they have made great improvement in a very short time, and I noticed with pleasure how bright, how eager to learn many of them seem."[10]

Forten also tutored adults in the evening. "Harry, one of the men on the place, came in for a lesson. He is most eager to learn, and is really a scholar to be proud of. He learns rapidly. I gave him his first lesson in writing. . .and his progress was wonderful. He held his pen almost perfectly right the first time. He will very soon learn to write."

Even on Sunday, her teaching duties did not cease. "Some of the grown people came in this morn. . . . This afternoon some of the children came in and sang a long time. Then I commenced teaching them the 23d Psalm, which Miss Murray is teaching the children in school."[11]

Teachers wore many hats, especially in the rural areas. They interpreted labor contracts, visited the sick, and helped the needy. In her diary, Forten described difficult, busy days:

Monday, November 17. Had a dreadfully wearying day in school. . . . Afterward drove the ladies to "The Corner," a collection of [N]egro houses whither Miss T went on a doctoring expedition. . . . Saw a little baby just borne today—and another—old Venus' great grandchild for whom I made the little pink frock.

The most radical activity in the freedmen's schools was the end-of-the-day singing of "John Brown's Body," about the white abolitionist John Brown, who was hanged for planning a slave revolt at Harper's Ferry, Virginia, in 1859.

Elizabeth Botume, another "Yankee schoolmarm," described her experiences on the Sea Islands in the early 1860s. Her schoolhouse was one large room without a roof but with six windows with panes in them, which was considered a luxury. The schoolroom also contained:

a few wooden benches, a tall pine desk with a high office stool, one narrow blackboard leaning against a post, and a huge box stove. The pipe of the stove was put through one window. . . . I believe this was the first building ever erected exclusively for a colored school. It was built for the colored refugees with a fund sent to General Saxton for this purpose by a ladies' freedman's aid society in England.

Botume wrote that the other freedmen's schools were "kept in churches, or cotton-barns, or old kitchens. Some teachers had their classes in tents."[13]

The schools were as varied as the teachers and the circumstances under which they were established. Some struggled because of lack of funds and competent teachers, and local hostility. Some schools were equal to the best New England grammar schools—the model for many of the freedmen's schools.

In 1870 the Freedmen's Bureau ended its work. The bureau was never intended to be a permanent organization, and Congress felt its mission was completed. Superintendent Alvord's final report indicated that 1,968 day and night

Fisk University in Nashville, Tennessee, was among the black colleges founded during Reconstruction.

The Jubilee Singers of Fisk toured England in the 1860s and were invited to give a concert before Queen Victoria.

schools, with 2,456 teachers and 114,795 black students, had been established in the former Confederate states. This was a monumental achievement.[14]

However, some black leaders and educators were critical of the emphasis on industrial education. Dr. William A. Sinclair, a black physician, believed that if black educators "had yielded to a 'craze' for industrial education," such a curriculum would have "stunted all higher and broader growth, and held the race closed down to the lines of hewers of wood and drawers of water."[15]

Also, by 1870, the aid societies and religious institutions began paring down their elementary-school programs. However, many black colleges and universities were founded in this period, with the goal of training black teachers to take over the work begun by the societies. Howard University, Hampton Institute, Atlanta University (started by two freedmen and a white AMA missionary in an abandoned railroad car), Dillard University, Clark College, Claflin College, Shaw University, and Fisk University all emerged in the Reconstruction era.

But in spite of the progress, the African-American journey toward full citizenship and freedom was far from over.

Brief Biography
CHARLOTTE FORTEN GRIMKE

Charlotte Forten Grimke

Charlotte Forten Grimke was among hundreds of Yankee school teachers who flocked to the coastal islands of South Carolina in order to educate the freedmen. Born into a prominent free black family in Philadelphia, Pennsylvania, on August 17, 1837, Charlotte continued a family tradition combining strong moral and cultural values with a sense of responsibility for helping others who were less fortunate.

The Forten family had been free for four generations. Charlotte's paternal grandfather, James Forten, served in the Revolutionary War, after joining the American patriots when he was fourteen years old. He became a sailmaker, inventing a mechanism for operating sails, and owned a successful business at a time when most free blacks were relegated to poorly paid manual labor. James Forten's invention, along with his business acumen, made him a wealthy man. He was, therefore, able to give his wife and eight children opportunities for education, travel, and cultural activities.[1]

Forten joined with other educated free blacks in the antislavery movement and in efforts to gain equal civil rights for free blacks. The Forten home on Lombard Street in Philadelphia was a center of political and abolitionist activity. James Forten took part in the black conventions held in the 1830s in Philadelphia and in a number of other northern cities.

Charlotte was three years old when her mother died. She was raised by her loving grandmother and her aunts in the Lombard Street home. Like her father, she was taught privately at home because of the poor quality of the segregated schools for black youngsters in Philadelphia. In 1854, when Charlotte was sixteen, her father sent her to live with an abolitionist family in Salem, Massachusetts, where young women could receive a quality education. Charlotte found she was the only black student in her school.

When Charlotte graduated from the Higginson Grammar School in 1855, the direction of her life became evident, as her skills as a poet and writer emerged. Her poem "A Parting Hymn" was read at her graduation, and another poem was published in *The Liberator*, an abolitionist paper. She became a member of the Salem Female Anti-Slavery Society in September, 1855.

Charlotte then entered the Salem Normal School to prepare for a teaching career—one of the few professions open to women. Teaching would be a way for Charlotte to continue the family tradition of helping to "uplift" her people as well as a way for her to support herself. Her faith in the value of education can be seen in her writing:

Let us labor to acquire knowledge, to break down the barriers of prejudice and oppression . . . believing that if not for us, for another generation there is a brighter day in store. . . .

In 1856, Charlotte took a teaching position at the Epes Grammar School in Salem, just before her twentieth birthday. Over the following years, she began her career as a teacher, writer, poet, and most importantly, a diarist. Her five journals give us a detailed account of nineteenth-century life from the perspective of a well-educated, privileged, young black woman witnessing the final days of American slavery and the Civil War, and then the period of Reconstruction. Her journals also offer interesting comments on Wendell Phillips, William Lloyd Garrison, Frederick Douglass, Harriet Tubman, and other famous abolitionists.

Although plagued by poor health, she continued to teach and write until she volunteered to join the army of schoolteachers going south to the Sea Islands off the coast of South Carolina in 1862 to educate the freed people. She taught on St. Helena Island, in a freedman's school, until 1864, when she returned to Philadelphia after her father's death. She then moved to Boston, and took a position as secretary of the Teachers Committee of the New England Branch of the Freedmen's Union Commission.

Writing remained an important part of her life. Her essay, "Life on the Sea Islands," was published in the 1864 May and June issues of *Atlantic Monthly*. Her translation of a French novel was published a few years later.

In 1871 Charlotte returned to the South. She taught first in Charleston, South Carolina, and then in Washington, D.C. From 1873 to 1878 she worked as a clerk for the U.S. Treasury Department.

In December 1878, at the age of forty-one, Charlotte married the Reverend Francis J. Grimke, born a slave, who became a pastor of the Fifteenth Street Presbyterian Church in Washington, D.C. In 1880 Charlotte gave birth to her only child, Theodora Cornelia. Unfortunately, the child died five months later.

From 1885 to 1889 Charlotte and her husband lived in the city of Jacksonville, Florida, where he was the pastor of the Laura Street Presbyterian Church. After four years, they then returned to Washington and the Fifteenth Street Presbyterian Church.

Charlotte Forten Grimke spent the rest of her days writing and helping her husband in his ministry. They had a loving relationship; they wrote and published essays together, and were both committed to missionary work. She also wrote poetry and raised a beloved niece, Angelina Grimke.

After a long illness, Charlotte Forten Grimke died on July 22, 1914, at her home in Washington, D.C. Her elegant words live on, however, making a unique community and a long-ago past vivid and real for us. She still "uplifts."

14. Beginning of the End

The whole South—every state in the South, had got into the hands of the very men that held us as slaves.[1]
Henry Adams
Freedman

Southern resistance to the changes wrought by Reconstruction was unrelenting. As the freedmen tried to move forward, great tides of reactionary forces pushed them backward. The beginning of Reconstruction was also the end.

Reconstruction was a violent and brutal period in American life. Violence had always played a central role in the South—the violence engendered by the slave system, where physical threats and punishments were inflicted on the enslaved population in order to maintain control; and the violence inflicted on the freed population. During Reconstruction, the violence became organized as the South attempted to dismantle the new state governments and weaken the Republican party.

After the freed population, next in line to experience the wrath of the former Confederates were the Union League, the Lincoln Brotherhood, and other Republican political organizations. Violence generated by groups such as the Ku Klux Klan effectively dismantled these organizations.

The Ku Klux Klan was born in Pulaski, Tennessee, in 1865; a secret lodge, fathered by six Confederate veterans. Members described it as an organization of "chivalry, humanity, mercy, and patriotism." However, its purpose was to terrorize the freedmen and any whites who associated with them. "By social and business ostracism of the white Radicals, by intimidation and any effective means of violence conceivable against blacks, by the purchase of votes of any sellers, and by glorifying the white race and especially white womanhood, the Klan grimly moved to wreck each and every phase of Radical Reconstruction,"[2] wrote historian John Hope Franklin.

MISS JULIA HAYDEN, THE MURDERED SCHOOL-TEACHER.—[FROM A PHOTOGRAPH.]

The Ku Klux Klan, the White Man's League, and other groups spread violence through the South. But there were protests against these groups. A Louisiana editorial writer reported a White Leaguer's murder of a young black schoolteacher in Tennessee, and condemned the outrage.

Five years later, the Klan had spread throughout the South, spawning similar organizations—The Knights of the White Camellia, The White Brotherhood—and conducting a reign of terror that weakened efforts to implement congressional Reconstruction.

On March 30, 1870, Congress ratified the Fifteenth Amendment, in an effort to protect the freedmen's right to vote. It states that the right to vote "shall not be denied . . . on account of race, color, or previous condition of servitude." Congress also passed a series of Enforcement Acts, to stem violence against freedmen by white gangs. In 1871, Congress passed the Ku Klux Klan Act, making violent crimes against an individual an infringement of civil rights, and punishable as a federal offense. If local authorities, many of them Klan members or sympathetic to the Klan, failed to prosecute hate crimes, then the military could step in. The writ of habeas corpus, a legal order that must be issued before a person is brought before a court, was suspended.

But laws are merely words written on paper if there is neither the will nor the means to enforce them. In their efforts to "redeem" the South from what they viewed as the shackles of Reconstruction and the dangers of black equality, white southern leaders used political manipulation, corruption, intimidation, and violence as weapons.

Congressman Richard H. Cain, a respected black Reconstruction leader in Charleston, needed an armed guard to protect him, his family, and his home. Local leaders were even more vulnerable. At least one-tenth of the black members of the 1867-68 constitutional conventions became victims of violence, and seven were murdered. Klansmen beat a popular black leader in Georgia because of his political activities in forming an Equal Rights League. In Alabama, a black man, George Moore, was beaten and a young girl visiting his wife was raped because Moore voted the Republican ticket.[3]

Fifteenth Amendment (adopted 1870)

Section 1.
The right of citizens of the United States to vote shall not be denied or abridged by the United States or by any state on account of race, color, or previous condition of servitude.

Section 2.
The Congress shall have power to enforce this article by appropriate legislation.

In full regalia, members of the Ku Klux Klan prepare to hang a white man who supported the Republicans. Federal agents appeared in time to prevent the hanging.

Whites shot up a Republican political rally in Alabama, and four blacks were assassinated. In the Piedmont region of South Carolina, 150 freedmen were chased from their homes and 13 killed when an argument between whites and blacks escalated into an attack on any black person in the area.[4]

The Klan went after blacks who were prosperous. An employee of a black landowner was killed by the Klan, perhaps to terrorize the landowner. Whites who sold or rented land to blacks or who purchased produce from them were also victims.[5] The Klan took night rides around the homes of white Republicans. A North Carolina state senator, John W. Stephens, an advocate for the freedmen, was murdered in 1870. Several "scalawags"—white Southerners in the Republican party—were killed in Georgia.[6]

When blacks defended themselves, the violence escalated. Freedmen in a Louisiana parish in 1873 feared that Democrats were about to seize the local government and took steps to protect themselves. With the help of black Union army veterans and a black militia, they drilled, dug trenches, and took control of a small town in the county for three weeks. Then, whites equipped with a cannon and other weapons attempted to seize the town. The town's black defenders were outnumbered and outgunned. When the smoke cleared, 280 black people and 2 whites were dead.

By 1874, labor unrest in the North coupled with an economic depression that lasted six years had helped to erode the Reconstruction process. Those who opposed Congressional Reconstruction charged that the Reconstruction governments were corrupt. There were corrupt and dishonest adventurers who came south, and native Southerners, black and white, who helped them. However, corruption during this period was not confined to the South. There were scandals in Washington, D.C., and in New York City, where "Boss" Tweed and his political machine stole millions of dollars, and where industrialists Jim Fisk and Jay Gould "conceived a plot to corner the gold on the New York market and to make millions by selling at the proper moment." There was no end to the schemes and scams during this period.[7]

Thomas Nast, a courageous political cartoonist, created this commentary on the collapse of the Freedmen's Savings and Trust Company.

Banking practices—making risky loans to businesses and moving "commercial paper from one bank to another for speculative purposes"—also contributed to the unstable economic situation. The Freedmen's Savings and Trust Company failed when Jay Cooke and Company, an investment firm, ruined the bank through failed investments. For years afterward, elderly black men and women tried to recover their savings. Other banks also closed. In many cases, government and business colluded, adding to the economic uncertainty and business failures. By 1874, more than 5,000 businesses had failed, and 89 railroad companies couldn't pay the bonds that they had issued to raise capital.[8]

In 1874, the Republicans lost their majority in Congress. Corruption and scandal threatened to bring down President Ulysses S. Grant's administration. Both the North and the South were war weary and Reconstruction weary. Northerners increasingly felt that the South should be left alone to settle its problems. By 1877 President Grant had pardoned former Confederates, thus swelling the ranks of white voters. With each election in the South, the opponents of Reconstruction gained more control of the state legislatures and dismantled Reconstruction legislation; redeeming their states, they said, from Republican and Negro rule.

As early as 1871, Georgia elected a Democratic governor. Slowly but steadily, the Democratic Party began to take the reins throughout the South. Along with violence and threats, other methods were used to control black voters. In some states lawmakers changed the voting qualifications outlined in the Reconstruction Acts and effectively bypassed the Fifteenth Amendment. Poll taxes, property qualifications, and literacy examinations limited black voters, the bulwark of the Republican Party in the South. (The regulations also kept European immigrants and the Chinese in the far West from voting.) Missouri, Tennessee, Virginia, and West Virginia enacted voting restrictions that worked against African-Americans. In 1874 and 1875 the growing number of Democrats in Congress, along with the new Republican leaders who did not support Radical Reconstruction, prevented the passage of laws that would have given the federal government additional jurisdiction over elections in the South.

It seems almost symbolic that Senator Charles Sumner died in 1874. He had waged a lifelong battle against slavery and racism, but his death signaled the beginning of the end of Reconstruction. In 1875, the Civil Rights Bill that Sumner had championed was signed into law. The bill guaranteed all citizens equal access to public facilities. Yet violence was reaching new heights. Mississippi descended into near-anarchy during the 1875 elections, when violence and fraud reigned. Congressman John R. Lynch requested that President Grant send troops to protect black voters. Grant refused; although he had earlier asked Congress to ban the Klan and other hate groups. The president believed that sending troops to Mississippi would worsen the situation. Grant felt that public sentiment would be against the government ordering troops into a southern state when the North and the South were trying to normalize relations.[9]

A year later, the president had to send federal troops to South Carolina to quell violence. One incident, particularly, signaled the breakdown of law and order. Members of a black militia parading in the town of Hamburg during Independence Day celebrations were arrested when they refused an order to stop marching. At their trial, they would not apologize, nor give up their weapons. Whites attending the trial opened fire, and five blacks were killed. Other militia members were killed as they ran from the courtroom.[10] The continuing violence and unrest in South Carolina led to the election of Democrat Wade Hampton as governor in 1876. Democrats also won gubernatorial elections in Louisiana and Florida.

Those in power can change state and local laws. As the Republican governments in the South toppled, the incoming Democrats rewrote some laws and ignored others. Labor laws were changed to give planters more control. Laws allowed landlords to claim their share of the crop, under the sharecropping system, before paying wages to the laborers. Sharecropping itself was redefined. The laborer and the planter no longer shared the harvested crop equally. The laborer worked the land, but the landlord owned the crop.[11]

In some parts of the South a new form of slavery—the convict-lease system—was created as prisoners were hired out to farms and industries to perform manual labor. Most of these prisoners were black, and many had committed only minor offenses, such as not being able to show a permanent address.

Election district lines were redrawn so that areas with many blacks were fragmented, to weaken their voting strength. The civil rights laws that guaranteed blacks equal access to restaurants, theaters, transportation, schools, hospitals, and parks were replaced by laws that separated blacks and whites in all areas of public and private life. Klansmen who had been

A Thomas Nast cartoon commented on Jim Crow laws that kept blacks from voting.

arrested under the Ku Klux Klan Act were pardoned and released. And the black Reconstruction lawmakers who were still in office in 1876 and 1877 were forced out.

Francis Cardozo of South Carolina was falsely accused of fraud and left office in 1877. Robert Brown Elliot was ousted from state government in May 1877.

In 1877, Republican Rutherford B. Hayes was declared the nineteenth president after a heated election. Hayes promised to remove the federal troops remaining in the South if he received enough electoral votes to win the presidency.

Sixteen years had passed from the first shots of the Civil War. Americans would put the war and Reconstruction behind them and move on to the industrial age. For African-Americans, the end of Reconstruction would usher in a long dry season of oppression and struggle.

This black family migrated west, built a makeshift cabin and staked a claim on land near Guthrie, Oklahoma, in 1889.

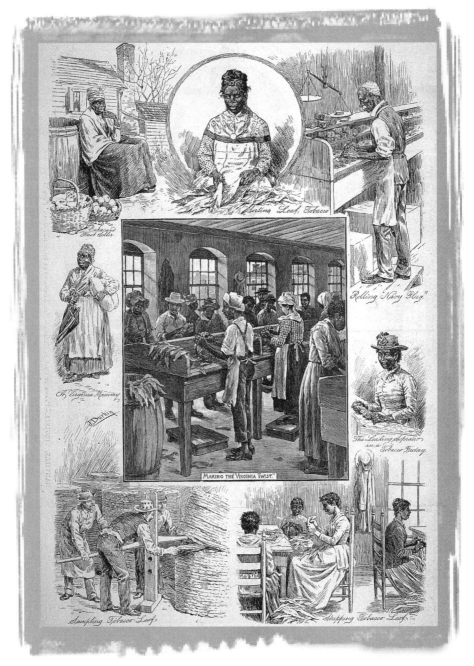

A Harper's Weekly *engraving showed the promise of Emancipation.*

Epilogue

Reconstruction did not end with a curtain dropping as when a play is over. A few remnants of the era lingered into the 1880s and 1890s. Some black Reconstruction lawmakers, such as John R. Lynch, remained active in Republican politics. He was elected to Congress in 1882. George H. White, representative from North Carolina, served in Congress from 1897 to 1901. He was the last black southern Congressman until Andrew Young of Georgia was elected in 1972. A few black men also sat on local city councils in heavily black areas, such as the low country of South Carolina, parts of North Carolina, and parts of Texas.[1]

The masses of blacks during the post-Reconstruction period did not fare well. The leaders and lawmakers of the "New South" did everything they could to keep blacks a landless and dependent laboring force. However, men and women who had survived enslavement survived American apartheid. By 1879, thousands of freedmen had left the South for the West, especially Kansas. Others emigrated to Liberia, a colony in West Africa established for the resettlement of African-Americans. Those who remained amid the cotton fields and canebrakes of the southern United States turned inward, drawing on their strong spirits and wills. They built churches, established self-help organizations, and supported their schools and colleges. Out of an African past and an American present, they forged a culture that offered sustenance and hope.

The work begun during Reconstruction was not completed until the civil rights movement of the 1950s and 1960s when laws preventing African-Americans in the southern states from voting, gaining access to public facilities, attending schools of their choice, and enjoying the rights and privileges of other American citizens were finally erased.

Source Notes

INTRODUCTION

1. Lerone Bennett Jr., *Before the Mayflower*, 5th ed., (Chicago: Johnson Publishing Co. Inc., 1982), 29.
2. John Hope Franklin and Alfred A. Moss Jr., *From Slavery to Freedom*, 6th ed., (New York: Alfred A. Knopf, Inc., 1988), 53.
3. Bennett, 34-35.
4. Bennett, 35.
5. Vincent Harding, *There Is a River* (New York: Harcourt Brace Jovanovich, 1981), 27.
6. Joyce D. Goodfriend, *Before the Melting Pot* (Princeton: Princeton University Press, 1992), 119.
7. Benjamin Quarles, *The Negro in the American Revolution* (Chapel Hill: The University of North Carolina Press, 1961, 1996), 24.

1. A HOUSE DIVIDED

1. John Hope Franklin and Alfred A. Moss Jr., *From Slavery to Freedom*, 6th ed. (New York: Alfred A. Knopf, 1988), 76.
2. W. E. B. Du Bois, *The Suppression of the African Slave Trade* (New York: Schocken Books, Inc., 1969, original publication 1896), 54-55.
3. Du Bois, 56.
4. Du Bois, 56.
5. Du Bois, 55.
6. Mary Beth Norton, et al., *A People and a Nation* (Boston: Houghton Mifflin Company, 1986), 361.
7. Norton, 371.
8. Norton, 399.

9. W. E. B. Du Bois, *Black Reconstruction in America, 1860-1880* (New York: Atheneum, 1992), 58.
10. Du Bois, 79.

BRIEF BIOGRAPHY - PHILLIS WHEATLEY

1. L. Maria Child, *The Freedmen's Book* (Boston: Ticknor and Fields, 1865), 86.
2. Child, 87.
3. Child, 87.

2. FREE AT LAST

1. Mrs. Nicholas Ware Eppes, *Negro of the Old South* (Chicago: Joseph G. Branch Publishing Co., 1925), 132-34.
2. Leon F. Litwack, *Been in the Storm So Long* (New York: Alfred A. Knopf, 1979), 319-321.
3. Litwack, 324.
4. Eric Foner, *Reconstruction: America's Unfinished Revolution* (New York: Harper and Row, 1988), 81.
5. Norman R. Yetman, *Voices from Slavery* (New York: Holt, Rinehart and Winston, 1970), 34.

BRIEF BIOGRAPHY - FREDERICK DOUGLASS

1. Frederick Douglass, *Narrative of the Life of Frederick Douglass* (New York: Signet Books, 1968), 53.
2. William S. McFeely, *Frederick Douglass* (New York: Simon and Schuster, 1991), 88.
3. McFeely, 117.
4. Mary Beth Norton, et al. *A People and a Nation* (Boston: Houghton Mifflin, 1986), 290.
5. Norton, 291.
6. Norton, 290.
7. Philip S. Foner and George E. Walker, eds., *Proceedings of the Black*

National and State Conventions, 1865-1900 Vol. I (Philadelphia: Temple University Press,1986), 24-30.

3. TIES THAT BIND

1. Norman R. Yetman, *Voices from Slavery* (New York: Holt, Rinehart and Winston,1970), 19-21
2. Henry William Ravenel, *The Private Journal of Henry William Ravenel, 1859-1887*, Arney Robinson Childs, ed. (Columbia: University of South Carolina Press, 1947), 218.
3. Leon F. Litwack, *Been in the Storm So Long* (New York: Alfred A. Knopf, 1979), 249-250.
4. Litwack, 250-251.
5. Litwack, 208.
6. Litwack, 208.
7. Litwack, 256.
8. Litwack, 257.

4. THE COMING DAY

1. Charles Joyner, *Down by the Riverside* (Urbana: University of Illinois Press, 1984), 137.
2. Elizabeth Hyde Botume, *First Days Amongst the Contrabands* (Boston: Lee and Shepard, 1893. Reprint, New York: Arno Press, 1968), 157-158.
3. Joyner, 217.
4. Frederick Douglass, *Narrative of the Life of Frederick Douglass* (New York: Signet Books, 1968), 114.
5. Leon F. Litwack, *Been in the Storm So Long* (New York: Alfred A. Knopf, 1979), 200.
6. Litwack, 333.
7. Norman R. Yetman, *Voices from Slavery* (New York: Holt, Rinehart and Winston, 1970), 225-226.
8. Yetman, 226.

BRIEF BIOGRAPHY - W. E. B. DU BOIS

1. Shirley Graham Du Bois, *Du Bois: A Pictorial Biography* (Chicago: Johnson Publishing Co., Inc., 1978), 8.
2. William L. Andrews, *The Oxford Companion to African American Literature* (New York: Oxford University Press, Inc., 1997), 237.
3. W. E. B. Du Bois, *Souls of Black Folk* (New York: The New American Library, 1982), 23.
4. Graham Du Bois, 155.

5. THE FREEDMEN'S BUREAU

1. Eric Foner, *Reconstruction: America's Unfinished Revolution* (New York: Harper and Row, 1988), 69.
2. W. E. B. Du Bois, *Black Reconstruction in America, 1860-1880* (New York: Atheneum, 1992), 223.
3. Barry A. Crouch, *The Freedmen's Bureau and Black Texans* (Austin: University of Texas Press, 1992), xiv.
4. Robert C. Morris, *Reading, 'Riting and Reconstruction* (Chicago: The University of Chicago Press, 1981), 34-35.
5. *Report of Refugees, Freedmen and Abandoned Lands*, North Carolina, 1866, 38.
6. Foner, 168.
7. *Report*, 17-18.
8. Crouch, 13-14.
9. Crouch, 107-108.
10. Crouch, 108.
11. Crouch, 108-110.
12. Crouch, 107.
13. *Report*, 35-36.
14. *Report*, 16.
15. *Report*, 19.
16. *Report*, 16.

17. Leon F. Litwack, *Been in the Storm So Long* (New York: Alfred A. Knopf, 1979), 439.

18. Litwack, 438; Foner, 70.

19. Vincent Harding, *There Is a River* (New York: Harcourt Brace Jovanovich, 1981), 318-319.

20. Harding, 321.

21. John Hope Franklin, *From Slavery to Freedom*, 6th ed. (New York: Alfred A. Knopf, 1988), 209-210.

BRIEF BIOGRAPHY - MARTIN R. DELANY

1. Frank [Frances] A. Rollin, *Life and Public Services of Martin R. Delany* (Boston: Lee and Shepard, 1883. Reprint, New York: The Schomburg Library of Nineteenth Century Black Women Writers, Oxford University Press, 1991),15-17.

2. Eric Foner, *Freedom's Lawmakers* (Baton Rouge: Louisiana State University Press, 1996), 59.

3. Foner, 60.

4. Carter G. Woodson, ed., *The Mind of the Negro as Reflected in Letters Written During the Crisis* (Washington, D.C.: The Association for the Study of Negro Life and History, Inc., 1926), 293.

6. THE SOUTH RISES

1. W. E. B. Du Bois, *Black Reconstruction in America, 1860-1880* (New York: Atheneum, 1992), 151

2. Eric Foner, *Reconstruction: America's Unfinished Revolution* (New York: Harper and Row, 1988), 36.

3. Foner, 36.

4. Milton Lomask, *Andy Johnson: the Tailor Who Became President* (New York: Farrar, Straus & Giroux, 1962), 110.

5. Lomask, 102-103.

6. Du Bois, 244-245.

7. Du Bois, 242.

8. Du Bois, 251-252.
9. Foner, 73.
10. Du Bois, 254.
11. Du Bois, 255.
12. Du Bois, 253.

7. ONE MORE RIVER TO CROSS

1. W. E. B. Du Bois, *Black Reconstruction in America, 1860–1880* (New York: Atheneum, 1992), 168, 170.
2. Du Bois, 170.
3. Du Bois, 169.
4. Du Bois, 173-174.
5. Du Bois, 177-178.
6. Du Bois, 170.
7. Du Bois, 141, 170.
8. Norman R. Yetman, *Voices from Slavery* (New York: Holt Rinehart and Winston, 1970), 226.
9. Leon F. Litwack, *Been in the Storm So Long* (New York: Alfred A. Knopf, 1979), 357.
10. Du Bois, 142.

8. NEW BATTLES

1. Eric Foner, *Reconstruction: America's Unfinished Revolution* (New York: Harper and Row, 1988), 240; W. E. B. Du Bois, *Black Reconstruction in America, 1860-1880* (New York: Atheneum, 1992), 261.
2. Foner, 239.
3. Du Bois, 257.
4. W. E. B. Du Bois, 262.
5. John Hope Franklin, *Reconstruction After the Civil War*, 2nd ed. (Chicago: University of Chicago Press, 1995), 57-58; Du Bois, 261.
6. Franklin, 58.
7. Franklin, 58-59.

8. Philip S. Foner and George E. Walker, eds., *Proceedings of the Black National and State Conventions, 1865-1900*, Vol. I (Philadelphia: Temple University Press, 1986), 112-113.

9. Foner and Walker, 180.

10. Philip S. Foner and George E. Walker, eds., *Proceedings of the Black State Conventions, 1840-1865*, Vol. II (Philadelphia: Temple University Press, 1980), 302.

11. Eric Foner, 230.

12. Franklin, 60.

13. Eric Foner, 230.

14. Du Bois, 193

15. Du Bois, 193.

16. Foner and Walker, eds., *Proceedings of the Black National and State Conventions, 1865-1900*, Vol. I, 214.

17. Foner and Walker, 217.

18. Foner and Walker, 220.

9. CONGRESS ACTS

1. John Hope Franklin, *Reconstruction After the Civil War*, 6th ed. (Chicago: University of Chicago Press, 1961), 60.

2. W. E. B. Du Bois, *Black Reconstruction in America, 1860-1880* (New York: Atheneum, 1992), 282.

3. Franklin, 62.

4. Leon F. Litwack, *Been in the Storm So Long* (New York: Alfred A. Knopf, 1979), 306. Franklin, 63.

5. Litwack, 306.

6. Du Bois, 272.

7. T. J. Stiles, ed., *In Their Own Words* (New York: The Berkley Publishing Group, 1997), 32.

8. Franklin, 66-69; Du Bois, 317-318.

9. Du Bois, 318.

10. Franklin, 68.

11. John R. Lynch, *The Facts of Reconstruction* (New York: Arno Press and

The New York Times, 1968), 17.
12. Franklin, 71.
13. Du Bois, 333.
14. Franklin, 74.
15. Franklin, 79.

10. THE NEW SOUTH

1. Leon Litwack and August Meier, eds.. *Black Leaders of the Nineteenth Century* (Urbana: University of Illinois Press, 1988), 105, 110.
2. Philip S. Foner and George E. Walker, eds., *Proceedings of the Black National and State Conventions, 1865-1900* (Philadelphia: Temple University Press, 1986), 40.
3. Foner and Walker, 41.
4. Foner and Walker, 41.
5. Foner and Walker, 67.
6. Foner and Walker, 40-41; Litwack and Meier, 114-115.
7. Foner and Walker, 68-70.
8. Litwack and Meier, 221.
9. Litwack and Meier, 223.
10. Litwack and Meier, 222.
11. John Hope Franklin, *Reconstruction After the Civil War*, 2nd ed. (Chicago: University of Chicago Press, 1995), 79.
12. Franklin, 79.
13. Eric Foner, Reconstruction: *America's Unfinished Revolution* (New York: Harper and Row, 1988), 317.
14. Foner, 318.
15. Foner, 288.
16. Foner, 320.
17. Foner, 325.
18. Franklin, 111.
19. Foner, 321.
20. Franklin, 104-105.
21. Foner, 333.
22. Foner, 342.

11. MEN OF THE PEOPLE

1. Eric Foner, *Freedom's Lawmakers* (Baton Rouge: Louisiana State University, 1996), xviii.
2. Philip S. Foner and George E. Walker, eds., *Proceedings of the Black National and State Conventions, 1865-1900*, Vol. I (Philadelphia: Temple University Press, 1986), 177.
3. Leon F. Litwack and August Meier, eds., *Black Leaders of the Nineteenth Century* (Urbana: University of Illinois Press, 1988), 209-211.
4. Eric Foner, 198.
5. E. L. Thornbrough, *Black Reconstructionists* (Englewood Cliffs: Prentice-Hall, Inc., 1972), 176-177.
   Eric Foner, 180.
6. Lerone Bennett, Jr., *Before the Mayflower*, 5th ed. (Chicago: Johnson Publishing Co., Inc., 1982), 241
7. Litwack and Meier, 201-204.
8. Eric Foner, 70.
9. Eric Foner, *Reconstruction: America's Unfinished Revolution* (New York: Harper and Row, 1988), 354-355.
10. Elizabeth Raul Bethel, *Promiseland* (Philadelphia: Temple University Press, 1981), 20.
11. Eric Foner, 356.

BRIEF BIOGRAPHY - JOHN R. LYNCH

1. John R. Lynch, *Reminiscences of an Active Life* (Chicago: The University of Chicago Press, 1970), 10.
2. Lynch, 42-43.
3. Lynch, preface.

12. EDUCATING THE FREEDMEN

1. Gerder Lerner, ed., *Black Women in White America* (New York: Vintage

Books, 1973), 28.

2. W. E. B. Du Bois, *Black Reconstruction in America, 1860-1880* (New York: Atheneum, 1992), 123.

3. Robert C. Morris, *Reading, 'Riting and Reconstruction* (Chicago: The University of Chicago Press, 1981), 1-2.

4. Morris, 6.

5. Morris, 13-14.

6. Morris, 14.

7. Morris, 36.

8. Morris, 16.

9. Booker T. Washington, *Up from Slavery* (New York: Dodd, Mead & Company, Inc., 1965), 19.

13. JOHN BROWN'S BODY

1. Robert C. Morris, *Reading, 'Riting and Reconstruction* (Chicago: The University of Chicago Press, 1981), 57 and 58.

2. Morris, 58.

3. Morris, 86.

4. Morris, 111.

5. Morris, 25.

6. Morris, 25.

7. Morris, 26.

8. *Report of Refugees, Freedmen and Abandoned Lands, North Carolina, 1866*, 37.

9. Morris, 178.

10. Charlotte Forten Grimke, *The Journals of Charlotte Forten Grimke*, Brenda Stevenson, ed. (New York: The Schomburg Library of Nineteenth Century Black Women Writers, Oxford University Press, 1988), 391.

11. Grimke, 398, 399.

12. Grimke, 399.

13. Elizabeth Hyde Botume, *First Days Amongst the Contrabands* (Boston: Lee and Shepard, 1893. Reprint, New York: Arno Press, 1968), 42.

14. Morris, 246.

15. Morris, 162.

BRIEF BIOGRAPHY - CHARLOTTE FORTEN GRIMKE

1. All information from: *The Journals of Charlotte Forten Grimke*, Brenda Stevenson, ed. (New York: The Schomburg Library of Nineteenth Century Black Women Writers, Oxford University Press, 1988), 391.

14. BEGINNING OF THE END

1. Eric Foner, *Reconstruction: America's Unfinished Revolution* (New York:
   Harper and Row, 1988), 582.
2. John Hope Franklin, *Reconstruction After the Civil War*, 2nd ed. (Chicago: The University of Chicago Press, 1995), 152.
3. Foner, 426-429.
4. Foner, 429.
5. Foner, 427.
6. Foner, 594.
7. Franklin, 145
8. Franklin, 181.
9. Franklin, 196-198.
10. Franklin, 203-204.
11. Foner, 594.

EPILOGUE

1. Eric Foner, *Reconstruction: America's Unfinished Revolution* (New York: Harper and Row, 1988), 591.

Bibliography

Andrews, William L. *The Oxford Companion to African American Literature*. New York: Oxford University Press, 1997.

Bennett, Lerone Jr. *Before the Mayflower*, 5th ed. Chicago: Johnson Publishing Co., Inc., 1982.

Bontemps, Arna, ed. *Great Slave Narratives*. Boston: Beacon Press, 1969.

Crouch, Barry A. *The Freedmen's Bureau and Black Texans*. Austin: University of Texas Press, 1992.

Du Bois, Shirley Graham. *Du Bois: A Pictorial Biography*. Chicago: Johnson Publishing Co., Inc., 1978.

Du Bois, W. E. B. *Black Reconstruction in America, 1860-1880*. New York: Atheneum, 1992.

_____. *The Souls of Black Folk*. New York: The New American Library, 1982.

_____ . *The Suppression of the African Slave Trade*. New York: Schocken Books, 1969. First published in 1896.

Foner, Eric. *Freedom's Lawmakers*. Baton Rouge: Louisiana State University, 1996.

Franklin, John Hope. *From Slavery to Freedom*, 6th ed. New York: Alfred A.

Knopf, 1988.

_____. *Reconstruction After the Civil War*, 2nd ed. Chicago: University of Chicago Press, 1995.

Garraty, John A. *The Young Reader's Companion to American History*. Boston: Houghton Mifflin Co., 1994.

Goodfriend, Joyce D. *Before the Melting Pot*. Princeton: Princeton University Press, 1992.

Harding, Vincent. *There Is a River*. New York: Harcourt Brace Jovanovich, 1981.

Joyner, Charles. *Down by the Riverside*. Urbana: University of Illinois Press, 1984.

Lerner, Gerder, ed. *Black Women in White America*. New York: Vintage Books, 1973.

Litwack, Leon F. *Been in the Storm So Long*. New York: Alfred A. Knopf, 1979.

_____and August Meier, eds. *Black Leaders of the Nineteenth Century*. Chicago: University of Illinois Press, 1988.

Lomask, Milton. *Andy Johnson: the Tailor Who Became President*. New York: Farrar, Straus and Giroux, 1962.

McFeeley, William S. *Frederick Douglass*. New York: Simon and Schuster, 1991.

Morris, Robert C. *Reading, 'Riting and Reconstruction*. Chicago: The University of Chicago Press, 1981.

Norton, Mary Beth, et al. *A People and a Nation*. Boston: Houghton Mifflin Co., 1986.

Quarles, Benjamin. *The Negro in the American Revolution*. Chapel Hill: The University of North Carolina Press, 1961, 1996.

Rollin, Frank A. *Life and Public Services of Martin R. Delany*. Boston: Lee and Shepard, 1883. Reprint, New York: The Schomburg Library of Nineteenth Century Black Women Writers, Oxford University Press, 1991.

Stiles, T. J., ed. *In Their Own Words*. New York: The Berkley Publishing Group, 1997.

Thornbrough, E. L. *Black Reconstructionists*. Englewood Cliffs: Prentice-Hall, 1972.

Woodson, Carter G., ed. *The Mind of the Negro as Reflected in Letters Written During the Crisis*. Washington, D.C.: The Association for the Study of Negro Life and History, Inc., 1926.

PRIMARY SOURCES

Botume, Elizabeth Hyde. *First Days Amongst the Contrabands*. Boston: Lee and Shepard, 1893. Reprint, New York: Arno Press, 1968.

Child, Lydia Maria. *The Freedmen's Book*. Boston: Ticknor and Fields, 1865.

Douglass, Frederick. *Narrative of the Life of Frederick Douglass*. New York: New American Library, 1968.

Eppes, Mrs. Nicholas Ware. *Negro of the Old South*. Chicago: Joseph G. Branch Publishing Co., 1925.

Foner, Philip S., and George E. Walker, eds. *Proceedings of the Black State Conventions, 1840-1865*, Philadelphia: Temple University Press, 1980.

_____. *Proceedings of the Black National and State Conventions, 1865-1900.* Philadelphia: Temple University Press, 1986.

Grimke, Charlotte Forten. *The Journals of Charlotte Forten Grimke*, Brenda Stevenson, ed. New York: The Schomburg Library of Nineteenth Century Black Women Writers, Oxford University Press, 1988.

Higginson, Thomas Wentworth. *Army Life in a Black Regiment.* Boston: Fields, Osgood & Co., 1870. Reprint, New York: Time-Life Books, 1982.

Lynch, John R. *The Facts of Reconstruction.* New York: Arno Press and The *New York Times*, 1968.

_____. *Reminiscences of an Active Life.* Chicago: The University of Chicago Press, 1970.

Ravenel, Henry William. *The Private Journal of Henry William Ravenel, 1859-1887.* Arney Robinson Childs, ed. Columbia: University of South Carolina Press, 1947.

Report of Refugees, Freedmen and Abandoned Lands. North Carolina, 1866.

Washington, Booker T. *Up from Slavery.* New York: Dodd, Mead and Co., 1965.

Yetman, Norman R. *Voices from Slavery.* New York: Holt, Rinehart and Winston, 1970.

Index

Page numbers in *Italics* refer to illustrations

About the Author

Joyce Hansen was born in the Bronx, in New York City. She earned a bachelor's degree from Pace University and a master's from New York University. She was a teacher in the New York City school system and a staff developer; taught writing and literature at Empire State College, State University of New York; and also found time to begin a distinguished writing career. Ms. Hansen and her husband now live in South Carolina, and she is a full-time writer.

Ms. Hansen has written fiction and nonfiction for young people, and her work has drawn both critical and popular enthusiasm and an array of awards. *Between Two Fires: Black Soldiers in the Civil War* and many of her other works were NCSS Notable Books; she received the Parent's Choice Award for *Yellow Bird and Me*, the African Studies Association Award for *The Captive*, four Coretta Scott King Honor Book Awards for *Which Way Freedom? The Captive, I Thought My Soul Would Rise and Fly,* and *Breaking Ground, Breaking Silence. Women of Hope* was selected as the 1999 Secondary Carter G. Woodson Honor Book.

973
HAN

Hansen, Joyce.

"Bury me not in a
land of slaves"

4157

$25.00